W9-DFV-487

STYLE YOUR *wedding* with NEIL LANE™

STYLE YOUR *wedding* with NEIL LANE™

Publisher Mike Sanders
Editors Ann Barton and Alexandra Elliott
Senior Designer Rebecca Batchelor
Proofreaders Lisa Starnes and Laura Caddell
Indexer Brad Herriman

First American Edition, 2019
Published in the United States by DK Publishing
6081 E. 82nd Street, Indianapolis, Indiana 46250
Copyright © 2019 by Neil Lane

19 20 21 22 23   10 9 8 7 6 5 4 3 2 1
001-313186-OCT2019

ISBN: 978-1-4654-8131-3
Library of Congress Catalog Number: 2019936936

Note: This publication contains the opinions and ideas of its author(s). It is intended
to provide helpful and informative material on the subject matter covered. It is sold
with the understanding that the author(s) and publisher are not engaged in rendering
professional services in the book. If the reader requires personal assistance or advice,
a competent professional should be consulted. The author(s) and publisher specifically
disclaim any responsibility for any liability, loss, or risk, personal or otherwise,
which is incurred as a consequence, directly or indirectly, of the use and application
of any of the contents of this book.

Trademarks: All terms mentioned in this book that are known to be or are suspected of being
trademarks or service marks have been appropriately capitalized. Alpha Books, DK, and
Penguin Random House LLC cannot attest to the accuracy of this information. Use of a term in
this book should not be regarded as affecting the validity of any trademark or service mark.

Neil Lane™; Rights of Publicity and Persona Rights: ABG-Lane, LLC. neillane.com

DK books are available at special discounts when purchased in bulk for sales promotions,
premiums, fund-raising, or educational use. For details, contact SpecialSales@dk.com.

Printed and bound in China

Contents

Dear Reader,

Congratulations on your engagement! Welcome to a fantastic and memorable moment in the lives of you, your partner, and your families. This period is full of love, joy, and dreaming of the future, and I am honored to play a small role in what is unequivocally one of the most exciting journeys you and your significant other will embark on together.

For over 20 years, I have had the pleasure of watching great love stories unfold. From engagement rings and wedding bands that begin a new and magical chapter to anniversary gifts that mark a life full of love, it is humbling to see the role my jewelry has played in milestone moments for countless happy couples across the globe.

Planning a wedding is an enormous task, and no bride or groom should have to face that challenge alone or unprepared. That is why I've compiled my years of experience and my passion for style and design into this book: to serve as a guide and a helping hand to assist you in creating the celebration of your dreams. In these pages, I have assembled practical advice, can't-miss planning tips, and a wealth of inspiration designed to inspire and excite you as you and your partner begin to fashion a wedding style that speaks to your aesthetic and your love story. We will explore six iconic styles— romantic, lavish, modern, elegant, rustic, and vintage—and the ways they can be brought to life through color, fashion, stationery, flowers, food, and more. On your wedding day, these pieces will all come together in a celebration that is effortlessly stylish and unmistakably you.

When it comes to a wedding, style is one of the first statements you and your partner will make together. Your wedding day should—and will—be beautiful, no matter which style most speaks to the two of you, and I am here to help make that happen. But style is more than just looks. It is the way you choose to celebrate, and how you honor and include the people you've invited to share in your celebration. The way you present yourselves, both aesthetically and emotionally, will set the tone for your wedding day and the years to come.

As you read through these pages and dream of the perfect way to celebrate this milestone occasion, always remember, in the end, it really comes down to celebrating love.

All my love,

PART ONE

THE IMPORTANCE OF STYLE

Style used to be a defined concept associated with specific women or men who were perfectly dressed in tailored attire, carrying themselves in a recognizable way. But as fashion and design have expanded beyond the luxury market, style has found a more fluid definition, and the concept of defining your own style has evolved. Today, style isn't just about what you're wearing; it's about how you're wearing it, and how the clothes make you feel.

That same concept can be applied to weddings. No longer a one-size-fits-all celebration with a poofy dress, baby's breath, and dry chicken on the menu, weddings can be customized to match your sensibilities. The colors, fashion, décor, and food can all be carefully chosen to create a mood and even an entirely new world in which your loved ones will celebrate.

The value of wedding style comes from the harmony it creates. Just as classical art turns to the Golden Ratio to bring balance to a painting, a defined wedding style helps a couple create balance and cohesion throughout their wedding day.

UNCONVENTIONAL CHOICES Modern weddings have permission to forgo restrained table settings, traditional lighting, and customary décor. Don't be afraid to make bold style selections.

FAIRY TALE CHIC Every choice, from the bouquet to the getaway car to the dress, speaks to your style. Consider how every element can make your dream come alive.

WHY STYLE IS USEFUL

As you work your way through the planning process, you will be called upon to make choices that will impact the look of your wedding, and thereby the way it feels. Narrowing down your wedding style by defining your vision will help dictate how those choices are made, creating a cohesive design from the save the date to the final dance. It creates beauty, but also has an important function—making wedding planning a little bit easier!

A defined style will help keep you moving in the right direction, eliminating extra options that don't fit and helping you stay on track. Creating a palette and selecting a style will also play an important role as you begin to work with other vendors. If you and your partner have a defined style, you'll be able to easily share it with each vendor, ensuring you are all working from the same inspiration and reaching toward the same goal.

THE BIG PICTURE

Style is most often associated with aesthetics, but that isn't the only thing that makes a person or an event stylish. How you treat your loved ones says far more about your style than any design decision you might make. Yes, your dress and your color palette may be high on your list of priorities, but showing love to the people you've invited should be at the top. It may be your wedding, but it's not all about you! A guest is a person who is the recipient of your care and hospitality, so prioritize your desire to show your loved ones how much you care above all else. With guests' comfort at heart, you will never have a bad event, whether you are hosting a wedding for 200 or a casual backyard get-together.

CASUAL ELEGANCE Consider choices that can help your guests feel comfortable, such as a family-style dinner. Putting your loved ones at ease makes it a memorable event for everyone.

MAKE MERRY The most flattering style is a high spirit. The planning must end when your day arrives, so let yourself laugh and soak in the time celebrating with loved ones.

HOW TO DETERMINE YOUR STYLE

Style is important, but how do you figure out what yours will be? Your wedding may be one of the first events you and your partner host together, so creating something that speaks to the two of you—while also being gracious hosts and welcoming your guests into such a momentous occasion—is of the utmost priority.

KEEP IT PERSONAL

This day is all about celebrating your union with your soon-to-be spouse, so fill your wedding with personal touches. Pick details that speak to you, whether it's a theme that really resonates, a meal you adore, or a palette filled with your favorite colors. Adding personal touches will remind guests whose wedding it is, helping them feel a closer connection to the two of you.

FIND INSPIRATION

Inspiration is most easily found in wedding resources—from magazines and blogs to Pinterest and Instagram pages—and those are fantastic places to start. These resources will have all sorts of style suggestions in the same place, and galleries from other couples' weddings will help you envision how every detail will come together.

Of course, that's not the only place to look. Nonwedding resources might really get those creative juices flowing, and a great team of vendors will be able to help you translate those ideas into your wedding style. Wander through your favorite museum in search of color palettes. Flip through a home design book or magazine for ideas about fabrics, textures, and even furniture pieces that might take your wedding to the next level. Pour over fashion magazines or the latest runway collections in search of silhouettes that could be perfect for your wedding day attire. If it speaks to you, it could be great inspiration for your wedding design.

"Have the wedding you love, because no matter how trends may change, the feeling of happiness and joy will always be there."

SIX KEY STYLES

While weddings come in all shapes and sizes, most fall into one of six key styles. These can be customized and made your own, but each provides a fantastic jumping-off point for a wedding that's true to the two of you.

ROMANTIC

If you've dreamed of a wedding out of a fairy tale, this is for you. Soft colors, flowing fabrics, and glowing candlelight come together for an enchanting evening that can be personal and intimate or dramatic and formal.

LAVISH

Lavish weddings are defined by over-the-top design, glamorous details, and lush embellishments. These celebrations are formal in nature, often held in impressive venues with large guest lists.

MODERN

Clean lines, sleek details, and sculptural accents define modern weddings, with restrained palettes and crisp pairings. Ornate design is traded in for carefully curated pieces and pared-down touches.

ELEGANT

This classic style turns to tradition for inspiration and will never look dated. Timeless silhouettes; effortless floral details; and refined, formal settings create sophisticated celebrations.

RUSTIC

Cozier and more intimate, rustic weddings pair refined details with natural elements like bare wood, soft flowers, and organic textures. Rustic weddings often have outdoor elements and are less formal in nature.

VINTAGE

Inspired by the past, vintage weddings embrace an era in all its glory—whether that's Art Deco, Victorian, or the elegance of the '50s. Details are a nod to the past, helping transport guests to another time.

DEFINE YOUR STYLE

As you're determining which style is right for you (and what your wedding day will look and feel like), sit down with your partner to answer these questions and give your wedding day a personal touch.

1. What are your top three priorities for your wedding day?

2. What are two details that aren't so important to you?

3. When you imagine your wedding, are there any details, rituals, or other elements you've always envisioned?

4. Is there a venue where you've always dreamed of having your wedding?

5. What is your favorite meal to share together?

6. What is the most amazing place you've visited together? What about a place that's at the top of your travel bucket list?

7. What are your favorite activities to do together?

8. What is your favorite item in your home?

9. What is your favorite piece of clothing in your closet?

10. Do you want your wedding to be more formal or more casual?

11. How do you want your guests to feel when they arrive?

12. What are things you've seen at other weddings that you loved? That you didn't like so much?

CLASSIC GRACE For the duo who feels most at ease with timeless details, choices such as white flowers, pearl jewelry, and restrained hairstyles will be pleasing to look back on even decades later.
INTIMATE SOFTNESS With organic accessories and fabrics that reflect the ease of nature, this couple has styled a wedding that evokes comfort and freedom.

FINDING THE RIGHT VENUE

Your wedding venue is more than just a room. The right venue will influence the overall style of your wedding, helping to set the tone and create an immersive experience for your guests. It can be a big piece of your design puzzle, or it can be a blank canvas upon which you create a celebration that's all your own. Whichever you choose, all wedding planning starts here. As you begin your venue search, consider these key details to set you and your partner up for success.

CHECK YOUR CALENDAR

Begin by thinking about when you want to get married. You don't have to set a date quite yet, but having a general idea of when you hope to tie the knot will help you determine a venue's availability, which will, in turn, help narrow down which venues you visit.

First, consider the season. Have you always envisioned yourself getting married on a lush, green lawn in early summer, or as the snow falls softly in the heart of winter? Use your wedding daydreams to identify a month or two that fit the bill. Resist the temptation to narrow down your potential dates any further.

Next, run this range of dates by your parents and siblings, a.k.a. your guest list VIPs, to make sure you don't sign a venue contract for the same day your sister-in-law is graduating from medical school. And don't forget to check your own calendars for any prior engagements you and your partner have penciled in!

Why such a large range of dates? If your dream venue is in high demand, you'll have better luck if you arrive at your tour with a number of options in mind. This will increase the odds of the venue being available on at least one of the dates you've considered, especially if you're planning to marry during peak wedding season.

PLACES OF WORSHIP If you have your heart set on a religious space for the ceremony, begin by getting a list of available dates here before you start inquiring at reception venues. **DESTINATION WEDDINGS** Dreaming of something further from home? Select a date that's far enough in the future to allow your guests time to plan for travel so they can be there on your special day.

BRAINSTORM YOUR GUEST LIST

You won't need a finalized list before you pick your venue, but you will want an estimate of how many guests you'll be inviting to celebrate with you. Start by sitting down with your partner and making a list of everyone you must have at your wedding. This VIP list should include key family members, as well as your closest friends—the ones who you'd dearly miss if they weren't included. You should each make a list of your own family members and friends, then come together to add mutual friends to make sure no one is overlooked.

From there, create a "nice-to-have" list. These could be extended family members, your favorite coworkers, or the people you know your parents really want to include—the ones you hope to invite, but who may not make the cut if your venue's capacity or your budget don't allow for a larger crowd.

Tally up both lists, then calculate 80 percent of the total. This will give you a general estimate of how big your ideal guest list will be once invitations are sent and some guests have RSVP'd "no." Take this estimate with you while looking at venues to determine whether your dream list will fit in your dream space.

SEASONALLY AWARE

If you plan to get married outdoors, whether close to home or at a far-off destination, you'll want to select a season when the weather will be pleasant and your guests will be comfortable. Off-season dates can be tempting, as great deals abound, but keep the weather in mind. Ask your venue representative about the average temperature, rain or snow conditions, wind, and mud— all of which can really put a damper on celebrations—as well as weather alternatives like backup indoor space or the use of a tent.

"You have your own style. Your wedding is the perfect opportunity to show it to the world."

HOW BIG SHOULD YOUR WEDDING BE?

Choosing whether to invite everyone you know or to keep things intimate is a difficult decision, but it's one that every couple needs to make early on. Knowing whether you'll have a big or small wedding will impact all of the major aspects of planning—determining which venues you'll look at, and how far your budget will go. While the perfect size guest list is different for every wedding, these pros and cons will help you find the right size for your celebration.

BIG WEDDING

Pro: everyone makes the cut. Yes, you'll still have to fit your guest list into your chosen venue, but deciding to have a large wedding means you can invite your favorite coworker, your cousin's kids, and everyone's plus-one.

Con: a tighter budget. You will, of course, have to feed all of these people! More guests means more meals, more chairs, more flatware rentals, etc., which could mean you have to choose less expensive options to make your dollars really count.

Pro: a packed dance floor. Large guest lists have a way of feeling instantly festive—especially when everyone is surrounding you and your new spouse on the dance floor all night long!

Con: fewer venue choices. While a guest list of 100 to 150 is still quite flexible, a much larger list (think 200 or more) will limit which venues can accommodate your crowd.

SMALL WEDDING

Pro: more time with your guests. Fewer guests means you will have more time to spend with each of them, so you'll get to create lasting memories with your loved ones and be attentive hosts.

Con: hurt feelings. The hardest part of paring down a guest list is deciding who doesn't make the cut. This can lead to people feeling left out, and you may have to defend your decision to have a small wedding to the ones who don't get invited.

Pro: more venue options. With a smaller guest list, you'll be able to fit just about anywhere! Just avoid spaces that are too big, as a room for 200 can feel empty with only 50 guests inside.

Con: high minimums. If your venue has a food and beverage minimum, that will apply even if you're celebrating with a few dozen guests. A smaller guest list won't necessarily save you money.

KEEP BUDGET IN MIND

An understanding of your overall budget will be crucial when it comes to picking the best venue for your wedding day—and there's more to it than just the cost to use the space. Venues range from basic blank spaces, where you'll have to provide everything from furniture to catering and waitstaff, to full-service sites that have the necessities such as in-house catering and basic banquet furniture included. Prices for venues (and those necessary add-ons) can vary widely from location to location, so research the average costs in your area to get an understanding of what your dream space will cost once it's all dolled up. As you're deciding how much you're willing to spend on your venue, remember these additional budget items that will add to your bottom line.

SPACE RENTAL

Rental fees are your cost of entry, giving you access to your venue on your selected date. Depending on the venue you choose, this might only include access and basic services, or your space rental could cover things like usage of the venue's existing furniture. This fee will vary widely depending on the types of venues you're looking at, from a more affordable town pavilion to an extravagant downtown hotel.

FURNITURE AND DÉCOR

How much furniture you rent will depend on your venue, as well as how dramatically you'd like to alter it with décor pieces. For example, a hotel ballroom will usually include banquet and round tables, as well as chairs, in the rental fee. You can save on rentals by using the included furniture, or opt to put a personal touch on the space by renting different tables and chairs. A more basic space might not include any furniture at all, so while you may have a smaller venue rental fee, your furniture rental costs will immediately be higher. The same goes for items like linens, dishes, and glassware—full-service venues like hotels or banquet facilities will include these items (though they may be very simple white china and no-frills flatware), but you might want to rent more design-focused pieces that speak to your wedding style.

CATERING

As Julia Child said, a party without cake is just a meeting—so what's a wedding without food? Wedding catering is most often priced per person, with a minimum dollar amount required for the evening regardless of how many guests you have. You'll see this per-person amount and minimum on a quote more frequently than a total estimate for your event, as your guest count will fluctuate up until the week of your wedding. If your venue has an in-house caterer, these fees will cover everything you need to feed your guests, including all the staffing. However, if you're looking at a venue that doesn't have a designated catering kitchen (say, for example, you're getting married on a remote ranch with no existing infrastructure), you'll want to talk specifically with your caterer about the items they'll need to build a kitchen on-site. This could include renting a catering tent, hot boxes, extra tables for food prep and plating, and a generator to power and light the tent. Ask your caterer if these items will be included in his or her fee, or if you'll need to rent them separately.

FEES, TAXES, AND GRATUITY

In addition to renting the space and paying for meals, your venue budget will need to cover service, gratuity, and taxes. These additional items are often denoted as "++" on your contract, either next to your rental fee or alongside the per-person food cost. Because this amount will change until your very final payment is due, as you make changes to menu selections and guest count, it isn't always calculated up front. However, it can really add up and catches many couples off guard. For example, if your venue rental is $10,000, the service fee is 20 percent, and taxes are 7.8 percent, you'll actually owe $12,780 at the end of the day—a difference of nearly $3,000! To avoid any surprises, ask your venue to walk you through any fees and help you estimate the total, then include a line on your budget to account for this additional expense in advance. Talk to your vendors about whether they include gratuities in their fees. For example, does the catering company's service fee cover tips for the servers and bartenders? If not, set aside additional funds to tip the team that will make it all happen.

FULL-SERVICE VS. A BLANK SLATE Spending more on a full-service venue might come with more inclusions (think in-house catering), so what seems like a steep price up front may save you in the long run. On the other hand, a blank slate venue might look like a steal, but once you count up all the add-ons, you could be in the same price range (or higher!) as a full-service venue. As you're deciding, keep your priorities in mind. If you're more focused on having amazing food and are happy with simple décor, designate your funds accordingly—whether it's to pay for a high-end hotel with a killer chef or to invest in an amazing local caterer. Are perfectly curated lounges at the top of your must-have list? Look for a no-frills (and low-cost!) venue so you can spend more on furniture rentals.

A BLANK CANVAS With room to accommodate a hundred or more guests, large wedding reception venues can feel cavernous and impersonal. Adding a comfortable couch, strings of twinkling lights, hanging floral arrangements, and fabric curtains can give large spaces a more intimate feel. Consider how you might use décor, furniture, and accent lighting to make your venue come to life.

TAKE A CLOSE LOOK
AT THE SPACE

When it comes to the style of a wedding venue, you have two choices: a venue with a distinct aesthetic (such as a tropical beach retreat or a rustic ski lodge) or a more neutral canvas (think hotel ballroom or a bare loft space). The style of your venue will impact the design and details of your wedding, as well as your budget.

A venue that brings a lot of details to the table will give you less flexibility to make the space your own, but you'll end up saving money on decorative accents because they are already included. That ski lodge, for example, might already have taxidermy on the walls and leather lounge furniture with nailhead details, meaning it will feel cozy and lived-in even if you only add a dusting of flowers.

Should you choose a venue that is a blank slate, you'll have much more creative license to transform it with furniture, décor rentals, and lighting—but that can cost you. Of course, you can also make a statement by keeping things simple and choosing select pieces that make a big impact, such as patterned linens paired with basic white china or the addition of one totally eye-catching floral display against a muted tone-on-tone palette.

UNCONVENTIONAL LOCATIONS
If you and your partner want to infuse a little more personality into your wedding day, there are plenty of out-of-the-box locations that are unique, exciting, and often overlooked as prime wedding venues. Foodies' mouths will water over hosting a reception at their favorite restaurant and, as a bonus, the cozy ambiance is built in. If you are art lovers, head to a local gallery or one of your city's most famous museums to give guests a taste of the place you call home. Outdoorsy couples can say "I do" in nature by reserving a spot at a National Park—just imagine how spectacular the photos will be. And if you're the bookish type, an iconic bookstore or stately library can give your celebration a literary twist.

UNDERSTAND YOUR OPTIONS

As you begin your search for the perfect wedding venue, give yourselves a head start in transforming it into the setting of your dreams by choosing a venue that's a perfect fit for your wedding style.

LAVISH

For a lavish wedding, nothing compares to the expertly styled ballroom of a gorgeous hotel. Chandeliers; gilded sconces; and a luxe, neutral palette will make creating your opulent celebration a breeze, while the accompanying high-end hospitality will have your guests feeling like royalty.

RUSTIC

Nothing says rustic wedding like a venue that has been softened by nature. A sprawling vineyard, with vine-covered hills extending beyond a quaint tasting room and cobblestone patio, would be relaxed, elegant, and welcoming.

ROMANTIC

Romantic weddings give off an unmistakable fairy tale ambiance, so seek out a setting that feels totally enchanted. A castle-inspired venue, complete with lush, flowering gardens and manicured grounds, will conjure up visions of a trip to Versailles.

MODERN

Clean lines and sleek shapes set modern weddings apart, and you'll want a venue to match. A trendy loft, downtown penthouse suite, or the halls of your favorite contemporary museum will set the tone for a no-fuss celebration.

ELEGANT

For an elegant wedding, a classic venue is the perfect choice. Head to a nearby golf or country club where you can exchange vows on the pristine green, then dance all night in the clubhouse.

VINTAGE

Vintage weddings are the best fit for venues that match the era of your inspiration. A historic home or building—such as an ornate City Hall or a refurbished turn-of-the-century mansion—will transport guests to another era before you've even started to decorate.

PLAYFUL LANTERNS A totally blank canvas, such as a tent, gives you an opportunity to make more whimsical style decisions. Hanging lanterns of various shapes and sizes make this plain canopied venue feel like a fantasy. **SPARKLING BALLROOM** This couple plays up the crisp palette of this hotel ballroom, with its beautiful monochrome textures, by using whites, creams, and golds in abundance. **SIMPLE CLUBHOUSE** Find ways to welcome the unchangeable features of your venue. If your chosen space has brown carpets and a brown ceiling, use simple brown furniture rentals that look natural in the room rather than fighting with it. This couple has softened the look of the ceiling with large drapes of white fabric.

PLANNING LIKE A PRO

No one understands the ins and outs of planning a wedding quite like a wedding planner. These professionals have seen it all and are invaluable resources when it comes to difficult design decisions or tricky family situations. While hiring a planner can be an investment and require a significant percentage of your budget, the value of a great planner can't be denied. Not sure whether a wedding planner or a coordinator is right for you? Here's what they each do and why they might be the right choice for you on your wedding day.

WEDDING PLANNERS

A wedding planner is all about the details. She or he will be on your team to address all of the logistics that go into a wedding, from prioritizing and maintaining your budget to setting up a timeline and even managing your guest list. On the day of your wedding, your planner will make sure every single detail is in place and keep everyone on time. If you're creatively minded and want a pro to keep you on track and help you execute, a planner is right up your alley. Looking for design help, too? Many planners also offer design services as part of their full-service packages, helping you pick colors, design centerpieces, and make your day look as beautiful as it is seamless.

WEDDING COORDINATORS

Coordinators provide similar services as wedding planners but on a shorter timeline, meaning you're doing the bulk of the planning yourself up until about a month before your wedding. Many coordinators will help you get set up with planning tools (and even provide some vendor recommendations), but then will be hands-off until those last few weeks. At that point, she or he will take over, double-checking contracts, helping you track final payments, and putting together a timeline so your wedding day runs smoothly. Then, on your wedding day, your coordinator will execute everything you've planned so you can enjoy.

WHY HIRE A PRO?

Whether you've got the budget for a full-service planner or want to save by working with a coordinator instead, having a professional who can help make things happen on your wedding day is invaluable. Knowing everything you've planned is in capable hands will allow you to relax and celebrate instead of worrying about whether everyone has a seat or the shuttles are late. It's an investment in your peace of mind—and that of your closest loved ones! That is worth every penny.

"Weddings are full of emotion—and more than a few nerves. Bringing in a professional can help ease that stress so you can really enjoy the moment."

CHOOSING A COLOR PALETTE

A color palette is the selection of shades and hues you'll turn to as you're making design decisions throughout the planning process. These colors will help guide your choices, tying together all of the details into one beautiful big picture. Your palette will create cohesion between all of your wedding elements, from flowers to paper goods to linens, and will give your design a sense of sophistication. As a bonus, it will also help make some of those design decisions easier, eliminating options that don't fit the palette you've set. It's really the foundation of your wedding style, so let's talk color!

COMBINE COLORS LIKE A PRO

There's more to picking a palette than choosing a few colors and calling it a day. A great palette will have a sense of harmony and balance, allowing the colors to enhance one another without clashing. Aim for four or five colors total (including those metallic accents), for a palette that is well-rounded but not too busy. There are a few steps to pairing colors that will give your wedding style depth and visual interest, and it's a lot easier to master than it might seem.

1. **Select Your Base Color**

    This will be the most prominent color in your wedding design and will really set the tone for your celebration. If you are envisioning a moody, dramatic reception, opt for a saturated color like a jewel tone. Having a wedding that's light and fresh? A pastel is the way to go. Consider your wedding style, as well as any prominent colors in your venue, as you are picking this base color so that each aspect plays well together.

2. **Choose Your Accent Colors**

    Two or three additional colors will help round out your palette, create depth, and enable you to layer different pieces to devise a look that's all your own. You might opt for different shades of the same color (such as lavender and mauve paired with eggplant), or create a high-contrast palette with colors from the opposite side of the color wheel (garnet paired with emerald green, or blush paired with steel blue).

BLACK IN THE TROPICS This wedding has a dramatic color scheme featuring black and deep green as the base colors. Taking a cue from the Southern California backdrop, accent colors in tropical hues of orange and yellow coordinate with the environment. Light, neutral whites lighten up the whole package, while varying shades of gold add pop and shimmer.

3. **Add a Neutral**

    A neutral color will add contrast to your palette, whether it is rich and saturated or light and airy. Choose one that matches the temperature of the rest of your palette (steel gray with cool colors, for example, or buttery cream with yellow and peach). If you've ever painted your home, you know that there are hundreds of whites to choose from, but a crisp white, soft ivory, or yellow-toned cream is a great place to start. There are also many shades of nude and tan, as well as a wide variety of grays, that can add depth to your design. The spectrum of neutrals has a darker side, as well, with charcoal gray, mocha, camel, and khaki, creating intriguing shadows. If you're a little color shy, the neutral you choose can play a big role in your design, taking over as your palette's base color with other colors used as accents.

4. **Mix in Metallics**

    While a metallic isn't a must-have, it's a fantastic way to enhance your palette and, of course, add a bit of shine. Metallics range from crisp platinum or darker pewter to warm gold or the pink tones of rose gold, meaning there's a perfect metallic for every palette. Look for one that corresponds with the temperature of the other colors you've chosen. For example, a blue-based palette would be beautiful with a shade of silver, while one that features warm peaches would look splendid with a pop of copper or rose gold. Or you can go totally glam and focus on metallics, with a single neutral and a pop of color to take your design over the top.

GET INSPIRED BY YOUR VENUE

If you're not sure where to start when selecting your wedding palette, begin with your venue. It can be difficult to hide colors that already exist in the space (think paint, carpeting, or other finishes you won't be able to cover or remove), so instead of fighting them, embrace them. Use other shades of the venue's prominent colors to soften existing strong colors and transform the palette into one you love. For example, if the ballroom carpet has a bold blue running through it, go darker with navy and pair it with ivory and blush, or go lighter with French blue and pair it with matte gold. This will help your wedding style feel as though it belongs in the space you've chosen.

PEEK INTO YOUR CLOSET

Another fantastic source of color inspiration? Your wardrobe. Grab your favorite items, whether a solid color or a playful pattern, and think about why you love them. Does the color combination bring a smile to your face? Is the hue particularly flattering on your skin tone? Use this as a jumping-off point to create a wedding day palette that is particularly flattering for you.

PLAY WITH YOUR FAVORITES

Of course, your palette should represent the two of you! Get inspired by your favorite colors, then play with saturation to find options that feel fresh and authentic. As you're considering your favorite colors, ask yourselves a few questions:

Do they occur in nature? Colors that are more prevalent in nature will be easier to translate into your floral design. For example, there are a nearly endless selection of flowers in shades of pink or red, while yellow and blue blooms definitely exist (hello, hydrangeas and daffodils!), but may be more limited in variety.

Do the colors work well together? If you'd like to include both of your favorite colors, make sure they fit easily into a palette together, whether as the primary colors or as accents. If you love fuchsia and your fiancé is partial to gray, you'll be able to weave these together by adding blush and ivory for a more romantic vibe, or burgundy and charcoal for a dramatic feel. On the other hand, if you adore eggplant and your significant other is all about the neon green, you'll want to tone down your choices and find different shades (like a softer lavender and dusty olive green) that work better together.

Do they work with your style? Most palettes can be tweaked to fit whatever style you've chosen, but some work better than others. Stark contrasts like black and white are instantly modern and may be hard to translate into a vintage wedding. A tone-on-tone palette, though, with varying shades of the same color can be woven into just about any style, whether it's primarily white and ivory for an elegant wedding, lots of saturated pinks for a lavish celebration, or layered neutrals for an elevated rustic reception.

REFLECTION OF NATURE This rustic and elegant reception space plays on the rolling forested backdrop with organic wooden furniture, trailing green centerpieces, and blue-gray table linens and paper goods to reflect the sky.

KEEP WITH THE SEASONS

Nothing gives a wedding a sense of place and time like a palette that is in tune with the seasons. After all, Mother Nature knows what she's doing. Now that you've set your wedding date, use the season to choose a palette that's totally natural. These color combinations are pretty—not tacky—and will make choosing flowers and décor a breeze.

SPRING

For a spring wedding, pretty pastels feel light and fresh. A touch of silver or rose gold gives a pastel palette a more elegant feeling, while contrasting with white or ivory keeps it classic and sweet. Or go modern and create stark contrast with a pop of black! If your wedding will be in late spring, weave in a brighter, more saturated color (like coral or a richer pink) for contrast.

Blush, Dove Gray, and Ivory with Silver Accents
French Blue, Dusty Rose, and Sage Green
Lavender, Mauve, and Slate Gray with Rose Gold Accents
Mint Green, White, and Black

SUMMER

Summer brides and grooms are greeted with bright and verdant splendor. A light and airy color combination will remind your guests of a summer's breeze, while a more eclectic selection has "field of wildflowers" written all over it. Don't forget a little white to make those colors stand out. If you're in the market for metallics, brushed yellow gold will fit right in.

White, Sky Blue, Peach, and Taupe
Blush, Coral, Orange, and Fresh Greenery
Sage Green, Ivory, Steel Blue, and Gold

FALL

As the season changes from summer to fall, embrace deeper and moodier tones. Use natural accents, such as slate or warm wood, to create a lived-in feel, and add touches of crisp copper to make these welcoming palettes a little more formal.

Fuchsia, Burgundy, Plum, Reclaimed Wood, and Slate
Burnt Orange, Mauve, Dusty Rose, and Copper
Navy, Olive Green, Mustard, and Peach

WINTER

Let it snow! With holidays on the calendar, winter weddings feel instantly festive. Rich colors create a cozy setting, while dusty pastels soften the winter chill. Opt for ombré pairings for a wedding style that's romantic without feeling like it came from your favorite holiday film. Or fill your wedding with sparkle—after all, it is a celebration!

Burgundy, Plum, Dove Gray, and Slate
Silver, Sage Green, Olive Green, Dusty Blue, and Denim
Navy, Steel Blue, Dove Gray, and Ivory
Gold, Rose Gold, Silver, Black, and White

spring

summer

fall

winter

CAN'T-MISS COLOR TRENDS

Enhance your wedding style even further by embracing one of these design-forward color trends. They'll make picking colors a little bit easier, as well as elevate your design to new heights.

PASTELS

Often relegated to nurseries or Easter frocks, these light tints are much more versatile than they appear. Using all pastels will give your wedding an airy and ethereal style, and the accents you choose can take your celebration from rustic or vintage when mixed with delicate neutrals, to moody and romantic when paired with metallics or a more saturated color. Choose two or three colors at most to keep the palette from feeling like a child's birthday party, using more than one shade of a given color for depth. Or give pastels a sophisticated twist by opting for their dusty cousins (such as mauve, eucalyptus, and dusty lavender).

METALLICS

Your wedding is one of the best parties you'll ever throw, so why not make sure guests know you're celebrating? An all-metallic palette is full of sparkle and shimmer, a totally luxe choice for a couple who wants their wedding style to really shine. Pair three metallics to keep some contrast in your design—rose gold, yellow gold, and pewter or platinum are a match made in metallic heaven. Mix in a bit of white or ivory, whether as plates and paper goods or in your centerpieces, to avoid metallic overload. Want even more drama? Add a single vibrant color (fuchsia is always a good idea!) as your floral color of choice.

"Incorporating color instantly updates classic design, whether it's an aquamarine in a timeless engagement ring or vibrant flowers in a simple centerpiece."

LAYERED BLUES Take a more subdued approach by using several hues of the same pastel, layered with patterned china. Relegate accent pastels to the lovely centerpieces. **A TOUCH OF GOLD** Metallics work with almost any color scheme, offering the versatility of a neutral with added sparkle and shine. Incorporate metallics in your flatware, typography, and linens for an extra luxe look.

JEWEL TONES

Jewel tones are all about drama, packing an intense punch that lets guests know they're somewhere special. Jewel tones are most often spotted at fall and winter weddings, but they're perfect for any couple looking to create a moody ambiance or add a bit of romance. Give jewel tones a tone-on-tone treatment with a mix of aubergine and plum, accented with a pop of blush, or create vivid contrast by using emerald, amethyst, deep teal, and magenta. Warm metallics like gold or copper play best with these rich colors, and the addition of a neutral like ivory or taupe will help keep things from feeling too dark.

TONE-ON-TONE OR OMBRÉ

With slightly more contrast than a monochromatic palette, tone-on-tone or ombré palettes take the one-color look in a contrasting direction. With tone-on-tone, go for minimal variation (think ivory paired with white or two or three slightly different shades of blue), and use a neutral accent or a single metallic for a pop. If you are dreaming of an ombré wedding, incorporate at least four tints of the same hue, ranging from a barely-there pastel to a deep, rich tone. Consider, for example, the pink evolution from blush and petal to watermelon, fuchsia, and magenta.

MONOCHROMATIC

A wedding that's all one color is anything but boring, especially if it's a color you adore. Monochromatic palettes are quite modern and can make a major statement. Whether it's all white, solely fuchsia, or a flood of dramatic black, turn to texture to help break it up and you'll never miss an accent color. An elegant woven or velvet tablecloth, high-gloss dishware, and matte paper goods can create a surprising amount of depth, even in the same hue! Play with flowers in the same color, using an abundance of varieties for even more texture in your centerpieces.

RICH HUES Bouquets featuring deep shades of orange and coral are set off by emerald and royal purple bridesmaid dresses in this autumn wedding. CARDS OF A COLOR An escort card display offers a perfect opportunity to showcase a tone-on-tone color palette, with individual cards gradually transitioning from deep pink to light peach. ALL WHITE This bright monochromatic scheme incorporates white into every element of the design. Hanging white paper fixtures tie into white linens, ivory chair cushions, white flowers, and white dishes.

A PALETTE FOR EVERY STYLE

Not sure what you like? Let your wedding style guide you toward a never-fails palette.
They're classics for a reason!

Lavish

Lavish weddings use saturated colors, rich textures, and some shine to create a luxe, opulent ambiance. Embrace jewel tones and add gold for shine and a lighter tint of the dominant color for contrast.

Ruby	Amethyst	Blush	Gold
Navy	Emerald	Sage Green	Champagne

Rustic

Rustic weddings have a palette that feels comfortable and lived-in, often accented with natural tones. Muted colors and organic textures create a cozy ambiance.

Dusty Rose	Eucalyptus Green	Dove Gray	Ivory
	Peach	Sage Green	Linen

Modern

Modern weddings are sleek and sculptural, with a palette curated to match. Crisp colors and matte metallics create contrast without the fuss.

White	Black	Hunter Green	Brushed Gold
White	Gray	Blonde Wood	Copper

Romantic

Romantic weddings are ultra-feminine and straight out of a fairy tale. The palette is soft and sweet with just a dash of drama.

Mauve	Blush	Burgundy	Ivory
Dusty Blue	Petal Pink	Pewter	

Elegant

Elegant weddings are classic, formal, and timeless. The palette is refined and sophisticated, with a subtle combination that blends together seamlessly.

White	Marble	Silver
White	Blush	Champagne	Gold

Vintage

Vintage weddings draw on styles from the past, and the palette can vary depending on which era inspires you.

Gold	Silver	Navy	Deep Teal	White
Nude	Blush	Eggplant	Sage Green	Ivory

DESIGNING PAPER GOODS

Your wedding stationery shouldn't be an afterthought. The paper goods you select will appear at key moments throughout your wedding, from the first save the date to the final thank you note, so it's important to choose a design that enhances your wedding style and helps tell your story. The feeling created by your wedding stationery is informed by the choices you make, whether it's a printing process, paper texture, calligraphy style, or the perfect finishing touch. Explore your options, take time to touch everything, and imagine the story you'll begin to tell from the moment your guests open the envelope.

THE BASICS OF WEDDING INVITATIONS

While there are so many ways to customize your invitation suite to fit your needs, style, and budget, most include the same basic pieces. These are the items you will be considering as you design your suite, as well as when (and how) to use them.

"Connection is important in everything you do. How you connect the invitations to the flowers to the china will really draw people in."

SAVE THE DATE

This is the first glimpse your guests will get into your wedding celebration. Usually sent four to six months in advance for local weddings and nine to twelve months before destination celebrations, these let guests know when and where you'll be tying the knot so they can mark their calendars and start looking at flights. You might also include the URL of your wedding website so your loved ones can find a few more details, like your registry.

ENVELOPE

Every invitation needs an envelope to get it to the right place! Most couples opt for simple packaging, with the invitation and inserts tucked into a single envelope, but some choose a more formal presentation and tuck the invitation into an inner envelope. The difference? The outer envelope features your guests' formal titles and addresses, while the inner envelope is address-free and uses first names only.

WEDDING INVITATION

Mailed eight weeks before the wedding for a local celebration and twelve or more weeks for a destination wedding, the wedding invitation contains all the key details for your big day: Who, Where, When, and What to Wear!

INVITATION INSERTS

Within the invitation envelope, most couples also include an RSVP card (paired with a pre-addressed and stamped envelope) that guests use to let you know whether they'll be attending. A reception card may be added for a more formal wedding. If you choose to use a reception card, your invitation should only include the ceremony details, then read "Reception to Follow" below. The reception card will have the reception's time, location, and dress code. Other inserts may detail the specifics of hotel room blocks, the itinerary, or an invitation to the weekend's other events (such as a rehearsal dinner or brunch).

INVITATION SUITE Consistent fonts, color, and layout unify this package, giving guests a first look at the style of the big day.

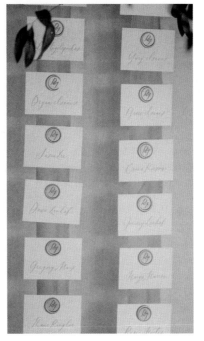

DAY-OF STATIONERY

The stationery for your wedding day should coordinate with your save the date and invitation suite, continuing the style story you've started to tell. It will help keep your guests in the know as they experience your wedding celebration, from the details of your ceremony to every mouthwatering morsel served at dinner. Each should be informative, as well as intentionally designed so every piece of paper fits into the big picture.

PROGRAMS

Ceremony programs will help your guests follow along with the proceedings. They can be as simple or as detailed as you like, but they most often include the order of the processional, the names of the family members and wedding party who will be walking down the aisle, and a brief overview of what will be included in your ceremony. If you like, you might also want to include the names of songs or readings, the text of important prayers, or brief descriptions of any traditions or rituals that may be unfamiliar.

ESCORT CARDS AND PLACE CARDS

Escort cards and place cards are similar in style but serve two very different purposes. Escort cards are displayed before the reception, and include guests' names and table assignments. These could be individual cards, larger signs, or a unique display that fits your wedding theme. Place cards are only used if you would like to tell your guests specifically where to sit at each table. They are quite popular for more formal events, but are less common if you're not having a black tie wedding. Place cards may be tented cards or displayed in place card holders, or you might instead opt to have each guest's name written at the top of their menu.

MENUS

Your guests may have already chosen between chicken and fish, but a printed menu will let them know what else they'll be served throughout the evening. Formal weddings often include a menu set at each guest's seat, while a more relaxed celebration might have a framed menu on each table. If you'll be serving the meal as a buffet, you could have individual cards describing each dish, or a larger decorative sign that walks your guests through all of their choices as they approach the food display.

LEAFY MENU The leaf motif is carried through all of the paper goods, including on the menu at each guest's seat. **REFINED PROGRAM** The simple and elegant ceremony program doubles as a fan to keep guests cool. **ESCORT CARDS** Creatively threaded on pink ribbon, these cards carry the same wax seal found on the invitations for this wedding.

HEAVY HITTING STATIONERY VOCABULARY

There's more to wedding stationery than hitting "print" on your computer. Different combinations of papers, printing styles, and handwritten accents can be layered to create a unique design that takes your wedding style to the next level. Whether you're going the DIY route or working with a stationer, study up on this vocabulary so you are ready to talk shop.

DIGITAL PRINTING

This is your most basic printing option and is great for thinner papers. Think of this as a higher-quality version of using your home printer—colors are more vivid, lines are more crisp, and designs are more detailed.

LETTERPRESS

Letterpress invitations are created using a metal plate carved away to reveal any letters or numbers in your design, which is then inked and pressed into your chosen paper (similar to a rubber stamp). The pressure of applying the ink to the paper sinks the letters into the paper, so you'll have slight recessed texture in addition to the inked text and design features.

EMBOSSING

Here, two plates are used to raise the letters out of the paper for a 3D effect. The main body of the invitation will include ink or foil so the details stand out, while blind embossing (which is three-dimensional but totally colorless) is used for borders or monograms to create subtle visual interest. The use of two plates means the back of your invitation will still be flat.

ENGRAVING

Engraving is the opposite of letterpress. The design of your invitation is engraved into the plate, which is then pressed down onto the paper. It will reveal three-dimensional texture,

but is differentiated from embossing because, when you turn the paper over, you'll see a slight shadow beneath the design that's engraved on the front.

SCREEN PRINTING

Often used for fabrics (think canvas welcome bags or monogrammed koozies), the design is created on a mesh stencil, or "screen," which is laid over the fabric. Ink is then brushed over the stencil which, when removed, reveals the design on the fabric.

FOIL STAMP

Similar to letterpress, a plate is used to press letters or designs into paper. Instead of ink, the letters push metallic foil into the paper, leaving a sleek and shiny design behind.

STOCK

This describes the thickness and weight of the paper. Lighter stock will be thinner and more flexible, while heavier stock will have a thick and substantial feel. Stocks also vary in texture, from linen and canvas to cotton. Thicker stock will work better with letterpress and engraving, as you'll need the thickness of the paper to allow the letters to be pressed in, while thinner stock is perfect for digital printing.

BEVELED EDGE

If you've opted for a thicker stock, you may have the option to add a beveled edge to your

invitation. Instead of cutting the paper at a 90-degree angle, the edges are cut on a diagonal to create a subtle point. Beveled edges are often painted or edged in foil for a sleek border.

DECKLE EDGE

This romantic paper treatment is the result of making paper by hand. Pulp is pressed into a mold, or deckle, then dried. When the deckle is removed, some pulp will remain along the edges, creating a soft and unfinished look. This unfinished edge is usually cut away, but leaving it behind adds lots of texture to an invitation suite. You can also get this look by using a ruler to help you hand-tear machine-made paper along a straight line. Nothing makes a deckle pop like a quick dip in watercolor paint or a little bit of hand-painted gold on the frayed edges.

BACKER

For a simple invitation, or one printed on lighter stock, a backer is a great way to add visual interest and a little weight. This piece of stock (in a coordinating color) is cut slightly larger than your invitation to create a border, then affixed to the back.

VELLUM

This translucent paper has a slightly plastic feel, but is sturdy enough to be printed on. It can be laid over traditional paper for extra dimension, used as a sheer

invitation liner, or inserted between the invitation and the envelope to help protect the invitation in transit.

LINER

An envelope liner is a way to add additional color or pattern to your invitation suite. Cut to fit into your envelope and then glued to the inside of the flap, this decorative paper enhances your invitation design, even if the invitation itself is kept simple.

1 Vellum A vellum overlay adds interest and dimension to your invitation suite. A layer of script softens an otherwise formal invitation, while colorful blooms frame a sweet and simple invite.
2 Foil Stamp Foiling adds a luxe touch to any style of invitation. Make a bold statement with all-gold foil on navy stock, or opt for glints of gold that highlight your invitation's design.
3 Embossing Subtle finishes can really elevate your design, like the blind embossing used to give this embellishment visual dimension. Embossing can also be used with ink to accentuate typed details.
4 Beveled Edge With the addition of rounded corners and foiled edges, this extra-thick RSVP card has edges cut at an angle, giving it a beveled look with extra depth.
5 Envelope Liners Liners come in solid colors or coordinating patterns to make the invitation cards pop.

1

Isabelle
ISABELLE GARDNER
&
ADAM FOX

SATURDAY, OCTOBER TENTH
TWO THOUSAND TWENTY
AT TWO O'CLOCK IN THE AFTERNOON

FIRST PRESBYTERIAN
120 SOUTHWEST ADLER STREET
PORTLAND, OREGON

DINNER AND MERRIMENT TO FOLLOW

WELLS
and
MARK DOMINIC
YOUNG

ask you to join them in celebration
on their wedding day

SATURDAY, MAY 16TH
two thousand twenty
at six o'clock in the evening

THE LAKESIDE GARDENS
16211 Southeast Foster Road
Portland, Oregon

Dinner and dancing to follow

2

FOR THE WEDDING OF

Margaret Eleanor
TO
Timothy Wright Jr.

SATURDAY, APRIL TWENTY-SEVENTH
TWO THOUSAND TWENTY
AT TWO O'CLOCK
IN THE AFTERNOON

Haiku Mill

250 HAIKU ROAD
MAUI, HAWAII

RECEPTION TO FOLLOW

3

PLEASE RESPOND

BY SATURDAY, THE NINETEENTH OF DECEMBER

4

please respond

before the tenth of september

m _____

_____ would be honored to attend
_____ number of guests
_____ send(s) best wishes

Hall and Timothy Wright, Jr.

8811 LADUE ROAD
LADUE, MISSOURI 63124

5

Isabelle Gardner
and
Adam Fox

request the honor of your presence on their wedding day

Saturday, the sixteenth of May, two thousand twenty
at five o'clock in the afternoon

The Lakeside Gardens
16211 Southeast Foster Road
Portland, Oregon

Reception to follow

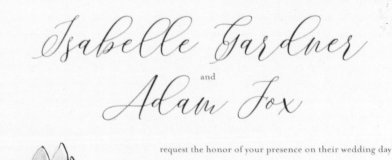

PLEASE JOIN

THE WEDDING

Margaret
&
Timothy W

RDAY, THE

MR. AND MRS. RAYMOND
proudly request your pr
at the marriage of their

Margaret
to
Timothy

CALLIGRAPHY

Calligraphy adds an artistic, handmade touch to an invitation suite, and there is a style to match every type of wedding. Calligraphy is frequently used to address envelopes and write names on escort and place cards, and can even be converted into a digital graphic so portions of your invitation suite can be printed in calligraphy that matches the rest of your paper goods. There are endless styles of calligraphy to choose from, and different calligraphers will each have their own signature fonts. But whether it is soft and flowing, thin and modern, or oh-so-traditional, these are the basic ways all calligraphy is created.

Mr. & Mrs. Edward Bill
425 San Clemente Way
Dallas, Texas
79046

COPPERPLATE CALLIGRAPHY

Copperplate script is a regimented writing style that is incredibly precise, but can be beautifully accented with swirls and flourishes. This iconic script is most at home on formal wedding invitations and will never go out of style.

The Randall Family
3345 Rowan Avenue
Raleigh, North Carolina
28764

MODERN CALLIGRAPHY

Modern calligraphy, on the other hand, embraces irregularity and imperfections, giving each calligrapher's style a look all its own. Modern calligraphy ranges from more formal—a softened take on traditional writing that is slightly more relaxed than copperplate—to casual lettering that might be big, flowing, and beautifully messy.

Jordan Frost
and
Caroline Beck
320 SAGE MOUNTAIN TRAIL
WIMBERLEY, TEXAS 78676

MONOLINE CALLIGRAPHY

Monoline calligraphy uses a felt tip pen to create thin letters that don't have the same thin-to-thick shape as pen or brush calligraphy. However, the range of options from different calligraphers means you'll still get lots of personality, in a more modern style.

THE HONOR OF YOUR PRESENCE IS
REQUESTED AT THE WEDDING OF

sara russel

AND

jacob arthur

SATURDAY, JANUARY 14, 2017
AT 4 O'CLOCK IN THE AFTERNOON
ANN ARBOR CITY CLUB
1830 WASHTENAW AVE. | ANN ARBOR, MICHIGAN

reception to follow

PEN CALLIGRAPHY

Traditional calligraphy is created when a metal nib is dipped into ink and used to write. This is most successful on smooth paper, as the nib can catch on paper that has a pronounced texture. Both copperplate calligraphy and types of modern calligraphy are written using this method.

Bryan + Kari

4353 blue spruce drive
north augusta, sc
3 4 2 7 4

BRUSH CALLIGRAPHY

Just as the name implies, brush calligraphy is created using a paintbrush, instead of a metal-nibbed pen, dipped in paint or ink. The size of the brush, the medium you choose, and the colors will all impact the results, but brush calligraphy tends to be softer and less rigid than pen calligraphy.

USING PAPER GOODS TO ENHANCE YOUR WEDDING STYLE

Paper goods may not be the first thing that comes to mind when you think about conveying your wedding style to your guests, but this oft-overlooked aspect of wedding design can carry some serious weight. Before they even step foot in your venue, your guests will get a peek at your vision through the save the date and invitation suite you mail to their homes, an invaluable opportunity to plant the seed for what is to come. All it takes is a little attention, some design savvy, and a few tricks to take your wedding stationery to the next level—putting your wedding day style front and center.

The first thing your guests will know about your wedding is what you put on your save the date cards, so take the opportunity to spread information and introduce your aesthetic. Use a font and palette that will correspond to both your wedding invitations and your décor, mixing in motifs that guests will spot later. For example, if you're marrying on a mountaintop, add a pair of skis to your monogram or top your save the date with a line drawing of a mountain range. Having a garden celebration? A border of watercolor blooms will hint at your design scheme—bonus points if you actually use those same flowers in your bouquet and centerpieces! The same goes for photo-focused save the dates. Use your engagement photos as an opportunity to set the tone, whether it's through your choice of setting, the colors you wear, or accessories that tie to your theme.

As you move on to design your invitations, use your save the date cards as a jumping-off point. Pick up that same typeface to create cohesion between each mailing and to keep the palette consistent. You may opt to have your wedding invitation be slightly more formal, with pared-down design elements and no photos, but weave in a few select details to create a cohesive invitation suite. You could nix the border of blooms in favor of an envelope liner featuring the same pattern, or use letterpress printing to give that typeface even more impact. And don't forget the invitation inserts. Repeat that floral pattern in the corner of your information or RSVP cards, and keep the typefaces consistent throughout.

When your wedding day arrives, continue the theme by again turning to those details you selected early on. Use the script from your invitations on the escort cards, feature your monogram on the cover of your program, or affix the same wax seal to the top of each menu. Consistency in design elements will ensure that your wedding style really comes through. Your guests will recognize the details you've chosen and be charmed as they appear throughout the night. It will also ease the design process for you and your partner, as you won't have to start from scratch with each round.

CACTI MOTIF Look to your wedding location for invitation inspiration. Illustrated cacti and succulents set a whimsical tone for a California desert wedding.

Turn to these same design elements as you collaborate with your vendor team. Bring a floral motif to life by using the same colors and flowers in your bouquet and centerpieces. If you used a playful pattern, find a printed napkin with the same design to add a pop to your dinner tables. If your envelope liner was a wash of watercolor, wrap your wedding cake in hand-painted matching fondant. These intentional and thoughtful design choices show you've truly embraced your wedding style on all fronts.

ESTABLISH YOUR AESTHETIC

Identifying a vision for your invitation suite will help you set a consistent tone, telling a story across all of your printed items that ties seamlessly into the rest of your wedding design. Carefully select typefaces, colors, and design elements that support your style, enhance your theme, and fit together to make a memorable statement.

FOCUS ON FONT

There is a wide world of fonts out there, and how you combine them will work wonders to enhance your wedding style. Traditional invitations use swirling copperplate calligraphy for key details, particularly the couple's names, then balance it with a serif font for the surrounding information. For a contemporary twist on this timeless pairing, swap in brush calligraphy or a more streamlined sans serif. Or give your invitations a dreamy vibe with hand block lettering and flowing modern calligraphy.

Use the same fonts on the rest of your paper goods. The serif or sans serif font is perfect for paper goods that present more information (like the body of ceremony programs or menus), while the calligraphy or accent font of your choice makes for beautiful headers, escort cards, or eye-catching signage.

And don't be afraid to embrace a theme. A single sans serif typeface would be perfect for a modern wedding, used everywhere from escort signage to bar menus. A rustic wedding, on the other hand, could get a playful pop from a more ornate serif font that subtly harkens back to the Old West.

GET COLORFUL

You've spent so much time selecting the perfect color palette, so start using it. Traditional invitations tend to use black, gray, or navy ink, but you can give a formal invitation a new spin by keeping the styling classic and opting for colorful ink. Color can also make an appearance on a painted edge or woven into your monogram or border. If you'd like to keep the invitation itself fairly traditional, add color with a ribbon, backer, or envelope liner, or choose a colorful envelope for a pop when your guests check their mailbox.

IT'S ALL IN THE DETAILS

You've chosen your fonts and played with color, but if you're craving a little extra detail, you're in luck! There are so many ways to give your invitation a little extra oomph.

One of the most common is a monogram, a combination of your and your partner's initials paired with swirling accents. Stick with just letters for a classic look, or take some royal inspiration and transform your monogram into a custom emblem. Surround the monogram with illustrated greenery and flowers, or add in miniature illustrations that speak to your relationship or your wedding celebration (such as bougainvillea for a coastal California wedding, a picture of your pup, or even an itty-bitty rendering of your venue).

Another option is to add an illustrated accent to your invitation. A border of flowers or greenery that fit the theme of your wedding will soften a traditional layout, while a slightly ombré watercolor wash can give an invitation suite a more artistic feeling.

EXPLORE ADD-ONS

There is more to an invitation suite than just paper. Creative add-ons will help you express your wedding style, as well as give your stationery a dose of personality. Whether you choose just one or play with a few, the right additions to your invitation suite will take it from informational to inspiring.

Ribbons and Belly Bands: To keep all of the pieces of your invitation suite together in transit, consider a belly band. This piece of paper, ribbon, or other textile wraps around the center of your invitation, holding any inserts and the RSVP card securely in place behind. This is an eye-catching way to dress up a simpler invitation, and the material you select will make your wedding style the focus. Paper or vellum belly bands are classic; dyed silk or velvet ribbons are soft and romantic; and twine or leather cord are unique options to make a rustic or masculine statement. Take this even further by tucking a sprig of dried herbs or a soft feather into the belly band to give your guests a multisensory experience.

Wax Seals: In the days of yore, a wax seal was a letter's mark of authenticity, but today it's an opportunity for couples to put their stamp (literally!) on their wedding stationery. Wax seals come in two styles: hand-applied seals, where wax is melted directly onto the desired surface before a stamp is pressed into the warm wax, or pre-made seals, where larger quantities of seals are prepared in advance and then finished with adhesive on the back, which you can then apply wherever you'd like. Use wax seals at the top of your invitation or menu in place of a monogram, to hold the ends of your belly band, or to seal envelopes. (This final treatment is recommended for inner envelopes only, as seals on the outside of your mailing envelopes may be damaged or lost in transit.) The seal can feature your last initial, your wedding date, or a small graphic that relates to your invitation design or wedding theme.

Envelope Liners: Even the most formal of invitations can benefit from a great envelope liner. This insert can add texture, contrast, or pattern to your invitation, and the options are nearly endless. Vellum or other sheer paper with a soft texture is a subtle finishing touch that helps an invitation suite feel polished. A colorful liner or patterned paper is playful and fun, whether it matches a motif on your invitation suite or further hints at your wedding's style. More ornate liners, ranging from hand-painted designs to bold metallics, become an aspect of the invitation suite all their own—consider using these same motifs on wedding day stationery to help bring it all together.

Mailer Boxes: If you are a fan of a more elaborate presentation, consider sending your invitations in boxes instead of envelopes. These boxes can be simple and sleek heavy paper, wrapped in luxe fabric, or ornate presentations like wooden wine crates. The box itself can play into your invitation design, adding another immersive layer of detail. The benefit of mailing an invitation in a box? All of the pieces inside are completely safe, and there's plenty of room for add-ons. Include vellum, tissue, or textured fabric to surround the invitation; layer inner envelopes and luxe belly bands; and include extras such as weekend itineraries or travel details so your guests are well informed.

Stamps: Embrace postage with personality. Wedding invitations are usually an unconventional weight, meaning you will need additional postage to get each invitation where it needs to go. Instead of piling on those American flag stamps, look for love and wedding-themed stamps at the post office that feature hearts, fresh blooms, or even wedding cakes.

For a more personal touch, consider ordering custom postage stamps featuring your photo, initials, or wedding date. Although custom stamps will require paying a little more for postage, they offer a special opportunity to personalize every aspect of your invitation.

If contemporary stamps don't fit your vision, enter the world of vintage stamps. Yes, you'll need more stamps per envelope (a 5¢ stamp won't help much if you need more than a dollar in postage), and you will pay slightly more than face value, but the combination of colors, illustrations, and sizes will give your envelopes a unique appearance that modern stamps just can't imitate.

GETTING THE LOOK

You've chosen a venue and set a date, so now it's time to figure out what you'll wear! Your wedding day will be one of the most-photographed days of your life, so you'll want to look your best—but that doesn't mean you can't let your personality shine through. Selecting suits, dresses, and accessories may seem like a tall order, but with a little know-how and a good dose of inspiration, you'll be beaming at that dressing room mirror in no time.

A DRESS FOR YOUR DAY

A wedding gown is more than just what you'll wear down the aisle. It can play a role in the overall ambiance you create for your celebration, a finishing touch that takes your design to the next level. As you're shopping for The One (gown, not spouse, that is), keep these three details in mind.

YOUR VENUE

They say you shouldn't pick a dress before you've chosen a venue, and they're right! It's good to know where you're getting married, as that will influence how your wedding looks and feels—and what you'll want from a wedding dress. After all, you don't want to fall in love with a heavy satin ballgown only to book a barefoot wedding on the beach. Think about the formality of your venue as you're looking at gowns so you'll be perfectly dressed for the setting.

THE SEASON

Wedding dresses can be comfortable, especially if you choose a gown and fabric that suit the season. Opt for lighter fabrics in warmer months (like charmeuse and chiffon) and something a bit heavier as the temperature drops (like satin or velvet). Think about the season when it comes to details like sleeves, as well. A soft and flowing sleeve may work great whether it's summer or winter, while a heavier sleeve might make summer brides sweat. And don't forget to consider whether you'll be indoors or outdoors.

YOUR STYLE

The style of your wedding will influence your dress, and the dress you choose will influence the event you design. Look for a dress that fits your wedding style (such as a dramatic ballgown for a lavish wedding or bohemian lace for a romantic celebration)—after all, if anyone should be dressed for the occasion, it's you! As you shop, keep your style keywords in mind and share them with your consultant at the salon. She or he will be able to help you translate the event you're planning into the perfect matching gown.

TIME IT RIGHT

Everything about shopping for a wedding gown is a little bit different than a regular shopping trip—including the timing. While some companies do offer off-the-rack wedding dresses that you can take with you when you leave the store, most gowns are made-to-measure, meaning they require significant lead time to be constructed to your specifications. Begin dress shopping nine to twelve months before your wedding date if possible, giving you time to visit a few different salons if you don't find The One right away. As you approach the six-month mark, you'll want to have your dress ordered so there's plenty of time for your dress to arrive and to schedule your fittings. Don't forget to tell your consultant at the bridal salon your wedding date so they can ensure your dream dress will arrive in time.

DRESS BASICS

No single article of clothing gets as much attention as a wedding dress, and with good reason: all eyes will be on you. The options for wedding gowns have never been so diverse, which can be both a blessing and a curse. With so many dresses to choose from, how is a bride to narrow it down? Arm yourself with basic dress knowledge so you can communicate what speaks to you, then prepare to walk down that aisle in style.

SILHOUETTES

Wedding dresses come in all shapes and sizes, but did you know those shapes have names? Brush up on a little gown vocabulary so you can better articulate what you like—and what you love.

a-line *mermaid* *short* *ballgown* *sheath* *trumpet*

A-LINE

An A-line wedding gown is one of the most popular silhouettes, and is universally flattering. This flowing skirt is full (but not too full), with a fitted bodice up top.

MERMAID

For more of an hourglass shape, turn to a mermaid gown, which is extra-fitted from the chest all the way to the knees. Va-va-voom!

SHORT

Not into ground-skimming gowns? There are a plethora of shorter choices, from a bridal mini to a sweet, tea-length skirt, as well as options for high-low hems to show off your shoes.

BALLGOWN

A ballgown is the epitome of a princess wedding dress. A fitted bodice sits atop a full, structured skirt that's begging you to waltz for your first dance.

COLUMN OR SHEATH

Brides looking for less volume love these simple shapes. Columns are sleek with a narrow skirt that falls straight from the hips. Sheaths, on the other hand, may have a slightly fuller skirt that still drapes delicately but has a more relaxed vibe.

FIT-N-FLARE OR TRUMPET

Show off your curves in a fit-n-flare or trumpet gown, which hugs the torso and hips (sometimes down to mid-thigh) before flaring out to a full skirt.

FABRICS

Don't get glossy-eyed when your consultant starts rattling off fabric choices. These are the most common fabrics used on wedding gowns to make sure you're comfortable with how your dress feels against your skin.

CHARMEUSE

This lightweight fabric has a smooth, satin finish and an easy drape. Often made of silk, charmeuse gives wedding dresses a slightly shiny finish and sleek style.

CHIFFON

Chiffon is a soft, sheer fabric that has an ethereal vibe. It is often used for overlays or sheer sleeves, adding a floaty finish.

TULLE

This gauzy woven fabric looks like netting upon closer inspection, and is sheer and lightweight. It is often used for veils, layered over skirts, or included to give a dress more volume.

ORGANZA

Organza is the happy medium between chiffon and tulle. It is crisp and sheer like chiffon, but has more structure like tulle. Flowy and slightly shiny, it is often used layered in skirts and trains.

JERSEY

This knit fabric is soft, stretchy, and a little bit clingy, ideal for simple, fitted gowns. It is supremely comfortable, but will hug curves and leaves little to the imagination.

LACE

This woven fabric flaunts intricate patterns that give a gown romantic detail. Often used as an overlay or an appliqué, there are nearly endless lace patterns to choose from.

SATIN

This traditional wedding gown fabric is slightly heavier with a noticeable sheen. It is most often used for structured wedding gowns, helping skirts hold their shape.

VELVET

A soft, thick fabric with a felted face, velvet is most often used for winter wedding gowns because of its rich, buttery texture and inherent warmth.

BRIDAL ACCESSORIES

With your dress chosen, it's time for those last few details that will make you feel like a bride. Whether you are donning a veil, adding jewelry for sparkle, or considering your shoe options, a few accessories will make your wedding day outfit complete. Once you have chosen your gown and veil, it's time to add jewelry in addition to your engagement ring and wedding band. You may want to add earrings, a necklace, or a bracelet to your wedding day look—but of course, you'll want them to fit the style of the occasion and work with your dress.

SHOES

Picking the right shoes for your wedding is crucial to both your look and your comfort, and is something you should think about sooner rather than later. You'll want to know if you plan to wear heels (and how high you're willing to go) as you shop for a dress so the salon can order the appropriate length of skirt, and you will need your wedding shoes at your fittings to make sure you can walk in your wedding dress without tripping.

When it comes to the style of your shoe, the choice is up to you. You may want to wear classic pumps in white or as your "something blue," block-heeled sandals for a sturdy step at an outdoor wedding, or even cowboy boots for a rustic celebration.

No matter what you select, break your shoes in before the big day. Wear them around your house, donning a pair of thick socks to slightly stretch the toe box if needed. Keep an eye out for places that rub and apply moleskin, a bandage, or a friction-preventing balm on the big day so you can walk down the aisle pain-free.

VEILS

Originally worn to protect brides from evil spirits, modern veils are synonymous with a walk down the aisle, and even nontraditional brides often opt to wear one—after all, when else will you get the chance? Ranging from light and incredibly sheer to slightly more opaque, simple to intricately embroidered, veils come in a wide range of styles. (And many dress designers even offer veils designed to match their wedding gowns.) If you've decided to wear a veil for your wedding ceremony, these common veil lengths will be the perfect finishing touch to your bridal ensemble.

BIRDCAGE

A few inches of open net or lace, a birdcage veil stays close to the face, giving your wedding look a vintage feel.

BLUSHER

A blusher covers the face and ends at the top of the dress, around the collarbone. This veil is often paired with a second veil, worn to cover the back of the head, and is lifted when the bride arrives at the altar.

SHOULDER LENGTH

Shoulder length veils give you the look of a veil without covering or competing with your wedding gown, approximately 20 inches in length.

ELBOW LENGTH

Elbow length veils are a great way to cover your shoulders during the ceremony without adding a sleeve or jacket to your wedding gown. These veils are approximately 32 inches long.

FINGERTIP

A fingertip veil gives you the noticeable look of a veil without too much length or bulk. A simple, sheer fabric will still allow for your dress to be seen through the approximately 40-inch veil.

WALTZ

At approximately 60 inches in length, a waltz veil creates a feeling of romance and drama, but is still short enough for you to dance comfortably without removing it—ideal for brides who want to wear their veils all night.

LET THE DRESS SHINE Pairing a sheer fingertip veil with a lace-covered gown allows the stunning mermaid flair to shine.

JEWELRY

Whether it's a simple family heirloom or a serious dose of sparkle, these are the small touches that take your style to the next level.

EARRINGS

As you're choosing your earrings, keep your hairstyle and the design of your dress in mind. You can't go wrong with a pretty pair of studs, whether they're all metal, diamonds, or pearls. They'll disappear softly beneath cascading curls, or catch the light next to an updo, and their petite size won't fight with an embellished bodice. Statement earrings are a fantastic choice for a bride wearing a simple gown who wants a dose of shine—just remember to bring them to your hair trial so you can make sure they don't get caught in your curls.

NECKLACES

Wearing a necklace truly depends on the neckline of your wedding dress. A higher neck or a gown with beading on the bodice may not require the addition of a necklace, while something more simple could frame one perfectly. You might opt to wear a small pendant or something that packs a little more punch. Just remember to try your necklace and earrings on together—if they are both statement pieces, you may want to skip one to avoid too much detail around your face or replace them with more subdued pieces.

BRACELETS

What about a little shine around your wrists? If you're planning to wear a bracelet or two on your wedding day, be sure to carefully inspect any clasps and settings (and have them repaired if needed) so pieces don't get lost. This is also important as a loose clasp can catch on fabric like lace or tulle, either getting you into a bind or potentially tearing the fabric. However, sturdy settings and clasps will go a long way in keeping your jewelry and your dress safe.

HEIRLOOM JEWELRY

Weddings are momentous events and often inspire loved ones to take out those special occasion pieces for your big day. Wearing heirloom jewelry is a sentimental "something borrowed," as well as a great way to include the people closest to you as you walk down the aisle and dance the night away. If the proffered piece isn't one you love, there are many other ways to carry it with you: a necklace or pin could be affixed to the wrap of your bouquet (as could a ring, tied with ribbon), or you could ask your seamstress to create a secure pocket inside your gown so you can carry the piece with you.

HAIR AND MAKEUP

A polished hairstyle and just-so makeup will go miles in making you look and feel your best on your wedding day, and it's all due to talented and trustworthy hair and makeup artists. If you have a stylist you already love, he or she won't just make you look your best—you will feel comfortable having them in the room the morning of your wedding, helping to make those early hours stress-free. Do plenty of research, reviewing stylists' portfolios and reading through reviews.

When it comes time for your trials, bring photos of looks you love (both from the stylist's portfolio and from other online sources—celebrity photos are great, too) to serve as inspiration. And don't be afraid to speak up. If a bun is too tight or the eyeshadow is too dark, use your trial as an opportunity to collaborate with your stylist to find the perfect final product. At the end, take notes about what was changed or what you'd like more of on your wedding day, and be sure to take lots of pictures as reference for later.

YOUR GRANDMOTHER'S JEWELS Whether they're from your relative's jewelry box or purchased new from the store, look for accessories that make your face shine, like these rose gold earrings replete with pearls and diamonds.

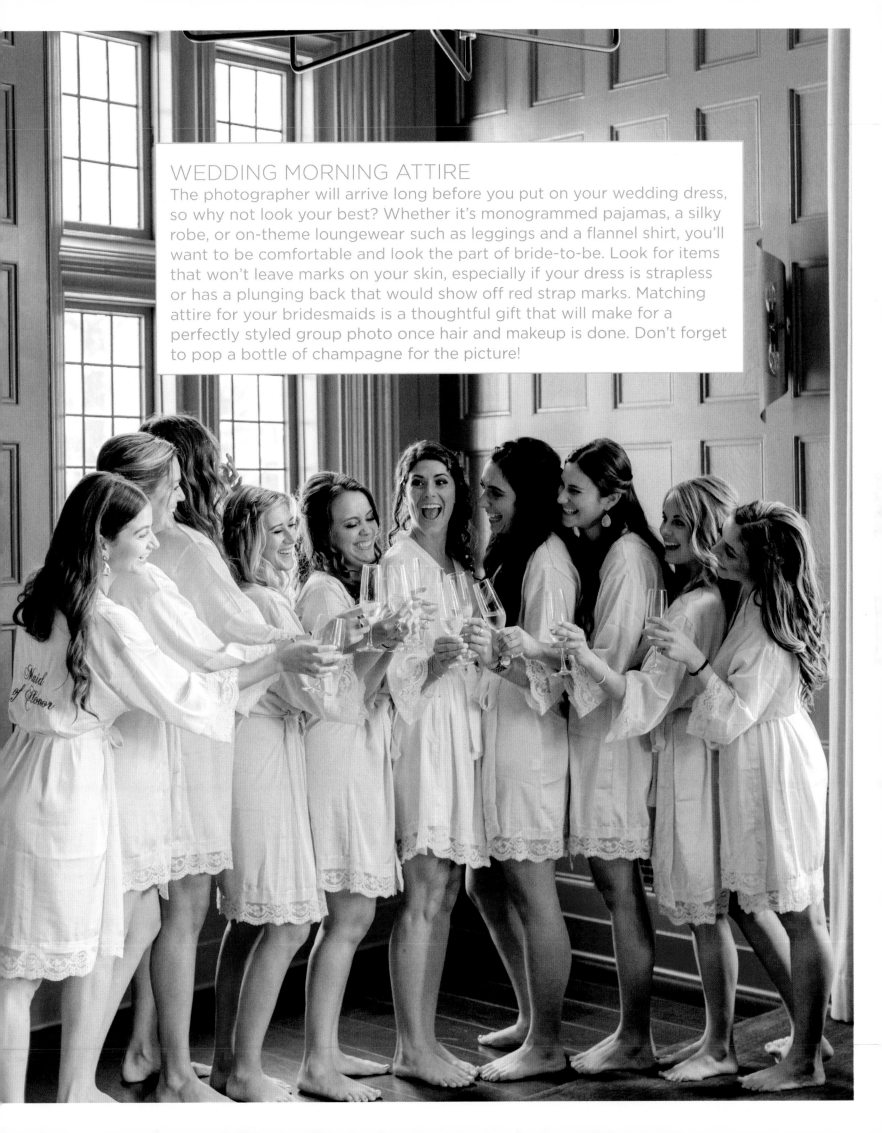

WEDDING MORNING ATTIRE

The photographer will arrive long before you put on your wedding dress, so why not look your best? Whether it's monogrammed pajamas, a silky robe, or on-theme loungewear such as leggings and a flannel shirt, you'll want to be comfortable and look the part of bride-to-be. Look for items that won't leave marks on your skin, especially if your dress is strapless or has a plunging back that would show off red strap marks. Matching attire for your bridesmaids is a thoughtful gift that will make for a perfectly styled group photo once hair and makeup is done. Don't forget to pop a bottle of champagne for the picture!

GROOM'S ATTIRE

Menswear is a world all its own, and while the wedding dress gets most of the attention, that's no reason that the groom shouldn't also look his best for his big moment. A carefully chosen suit or tuxedo will also go a long way in furthering the style and aesthetic of the wedding, paired perfectly with the bride's gown. It's all about knowing your venue and understanding your wedding style.

MENSWEAR BASICS

Groom's options for their wedding day fall into three basic categories: suits, tuxedos, and more casual ensembles. Each has their place, and a wedding style to match.

SUITS

If your wedding isn't black tie, men will wear suits—but there's a whole wide world of suits to choose from. A lighter gray is a handsome choice for a daytime or spring wedding, while darker gray or charcoal is an excellent choice for an outdoor evening wedding. Don a crisp navy suit for a romantic celebration, or go black with a simple white shirt and no tie for a modern wedding. And don't forget the lining. Add personality with a colorful lining, or have the inside pocket embroidered with your wedding date. Again, fit is key, so seek out a talented tailor—especially if your suit is off-the-rack and needs a few tweaks.

TUXEDOS

Lavish black-tie weddings call for a tux (or even a white dinner jacket if you're feeling extra formal). But this isn't the tux you rented for high school prom. Today's tuxedos feature modern cuts, might skip those shiny stripes on the pants, and offer a range of collar styles so you can put your own twist on your ensemble. They're also available in unique colors and fabrics (think a rich navy, a black tone-on-tone pattern with subtle shine, or textured gray). Shawl collars give tuxes a modern spin, while peak lapels are extra formal. Want to really make a statement? A double-breasted jacket (in a contemporary slim cut) will make you stand out.

CASUAL AND REFINED A perfectly tailored jacket in a lighter shade of navy is ideal for a summer wedding. Add an interesting pocket square that suits your personality, and you're good to go.

NOT YOUR AVERAGE TUX There is no question that a tuxedo ensemble is classic and formal. Make it your own with an updated cummerbund and bowtie in one of your wedding's accent colors.

CASUAL ENSEMBLES

This includes outfits such as khakis and a linen shirt (ideal for a beach wedding), slacks and a blazer (which has "relaxed, elegant wedding at the golf club" written all over it), and even jeans and a sharp jacket for a refined take on a rustic wedding. Even if you're opting for more casual attire, look for high-quality materials and invest in having pieces tailored for the perfect fit.

DON'T FORGET FABRICS

Don't forget to keep your wedding season in mind when selecting menswear. Pick the right fabric so you'll both look the part and feel comfortable, no matter the temperature. For a fall or winter wedding, keep warm in wool or add texture with tweed. In spring and summer, lighter fabrics like cotton, linen, and even chambray let you breath.

LAID BACK Is your wedding somewhere out of the ordinary—in the tropics, perhaps? Then your outfit should match. A simple linen suit in a pale shade of blue is perfect for this beachy wedding.

ACCESSORIZE LIKE A PRO

Every groom's look needs a few accessories, even if you aren't going full suspenders and cummerbund with your tux. The right belt, shoes, and tie will truly bring your look together. Most men opt to match their belt and shoes, and the same goes for your wedding accessories.

Brown leather is a fantastic option for a less formal wedding and can pair well with khakis or a gray or navy suit. Don lighter brown for a spring or summer wedding, and darker brown for fall or winter. If your wedding is more formal, opt for black accessories instead (which you can wear with gray, navy, or black). If you aren't wearing a tuxedo, skip the patent dress shoes in favor of traditional black leather—though you can skip it with a tux, too! Give your attire personality with a brogue or monk strap, or even a velvet smoking slipper for a high-fashion look.

Your tie can either be a classic finishing touch or can add a pop of color and personality. A traditional tuxedo can be paired with a satin or velvet bow tie (and now's the perfect time to learn how to tie one!). For a suit, a bowtie can also add personality, though you may want to swap the black for a print or color instead. If you are wearing a straight tie, use it to show off your style or keep things simple by picking a color that coordinates with the bridesmaids' dresses.

PATTERNS! Want to remain timeless while still infusing your ensemble with some personality? Printed socks are just the right amount of fun to amp up your outfit without going over the top.

WEDDING PARTY WARDROBE

Once you and your spouse-to-be are fully outfitted, it's time to dress your VIPs. Your wedding party, as well as your parents and siblings, will be photographed nearly as much as the two of you are, so make sure they look their best in carefully chosen colors and styles that fit your vision to a T.

BRIDESMAIDS

Choosing bridesmaids' dresses can seem like a huge task, but it doesn't have to be complicated. Begin by choosing a color, turning to your palette for inspiration. Bridesmaids' dresses look best in a softer accent color, one that will allow them to stand out instead of being swallowed by the base color you've focused on throughout your design. Avoid stark primary colors, opting instead for a softer pastel or a rich jewel tone. If you're leaning toward blush, keep skin tone in mind. Pink isn't "one size fits all," so you'll want to make sure the tone you choose doesn't leave some of your besties looking washed out.

If you're worried about finding the perfect color to suit every single woman, embrace the mismatched dress trend. This can be as particular or as relaxed as you like. Some brides prefer a curated collection of dresses, choosing two or three colors and styles and letting their bridesmaids each pick the dress that suits them best. Others would rather let their bridesmaids do the shopping, selecting a palette (such as blush, nude, and champagne) and setting a few design parameters so each lucky lady can pick a dress on her own. Another perk of letting bridesmaids choose their own dresses is that it allows each woman to spend an amount that makes her comfortable, which can be a welcome relief in the era of $300 bridesmaids' dresses.

More and more brides are outfitting their 'maids in fashion-forward styles, namely sequin gowns or floral prints. These allow the wedding party to have a little more personality, and are also a great way to have your maid of honor stand out amongst bridesmaids in a solid color.

The style of your wedding will come into play as you look at silhouettes and lengths. Floor-length dresses are more formal, while shorter frocks have a relaxed and casual vibe. Choose a slim cut or an architectural neckline for a modern wedding, or go for a flowy skirt or wrap styling for something more rustic. For a lavish wedding, look to luxe fabrics, and maybe a hint of sparkle.

GROOMSMEN

Groomsmen tend to wear attire that is similar to, if not the same as, the groom's, making choosing their clothing much more straightforward. The key is to focus on consistent formality so the groom doesn't look out of place in more formal attire than his friends.

It's an easy option to have the groom and his groomsmen wear the same suit or tuxedo. You can still differentiate the groom from his groomsmen with a different tie or a more interesting boutonniere. Alternatively, you could dress the groomsmen in something more classic (such as a gray suit or a traditional tux), then outfit the groom in a slightly darker shade of gray, a unique tuxedo jacket, or even a white dinner jacket, which would pop quite nicely amongst men in black tuxedos.

The age old question is: to rent or to buy? Rented suits and tuxedos have a bad rap for being ill-fitting and tired, but new online rental companies make renting a modern and fashionable suit for a single day as a groomsman relatively pain-free. This also ensures everyone will match, especially if you are asking groomsmen to wear a color other than black. On the other hand, most men would benefit from having a good suit in their closet (or may already have one), so your wedding could be the perfect opportunity for your groomsmen to make an investment. Even if you do go the rental route, purchase matching ties or other accessories as gifts to dress up the look you have chosen.

MATCHING DRESSES For a classic look, request that your bridesmaids don identical dresses, as well as the groomsmen. Options like these pale pink numbers have a modern halter neckline to update the elegant style, while the men are casual yet refined in navy suits.   **MONOCHROMATIC FROCKS** For brides who want to create cohesive texture, give your girls free rein to choose a dress that flatters and suits the budget. The bridal party will look put-together and clean while maintaining visual interest.   **COMPLEMENTARY SPARKLE** Hemlines don't have to match! Tell your maids that you'd like to see them in a champagne-colored dress with shimmer and glitz, and see what stunning options they unearth.

FAMILY

Keep your parents feeling like part of the gang in coordinated attire. Fathers can wear suits similar to the groom and groomsmen (and should also wear tuxedos if the rest of the wedding party will be doing the same). Set them apart with a unique tie or boutonniere—though everyone will know who they are, thanks to the happy tears!

When dressing the mothers, the mother of the bride should choose her dress first. She should dress in a color that coordinates with the bridesmaids, whether by donning a deeper tone of the same color or by choosing a neutral of the same temperature. Then, the mother of the groom should coordinate her attire with the mother of the bride. That might mean a similar shade or another color from the wedding palette. The mothers don't need to match, but since so many family photos will be taken, it's a good idea to choose dresses in colors that work well together.

Any siblings who are not in the wedding party don't necessarily have to wear particular attire, though of course they should follow the dress code. If you wish, provide them with the details of what the wedding party will be wearing so they can choose complementary colors and styles.

FLOWER GIRLS AND RING BEARERS

All eyes may be on the bride, but the youngest members of the wedding party will definitely garner a few smiles as they make their way down the aisle.

Flower girl dresses are often inspired by the bride's dress, a white confection with similar fabrics to give the young girl a princess moment. A sash and bow are great ways to add a pop of color, which can be coordinated with the bridesmaids' dresses. If you can't find a miniature version of your own dress, a tutu never fails. Send your special attendant down the aisle wearing a cloud of tulle and a flower crown, and she'll feel like a fairy.

There isn't anything cuter than a miniature version of a suit or tuxedo, especially as ring bearers tend to take their job as ring security very seriously. Choose a color and style that coordinate with the rest of the groomsmen for a ring bearer who is old enough to make the walk on his own. Younger boys serving a more honorary role look darling in more formal onesies, especially when finished with a tiny bow tie.

INCORPORATING PERSONAL TOUCHES

A stylish wedding is about more than beautiful décor—it's about creating a celebration that speaks to who the two of you are, both individually and as a couple. Incorporating personal touches will remind guests that they're at your wedding, celebrating a unique love story. Finding ways to include the things you love into the design, the menu, and the festivities will not only help tell the story of your relationship—it will create lasting memories that you and all of your guests will truly cherish.

Think about the things you and your partner love to share with one another. How do you spend your weekends? Where do you love to travel? What do you love to eat? What are some of your favorite shared memories? The answers to these questions can all be woven into your wedding celebration, giving guests a peek into your lives.

THE SIGNATURE COCKTAIL

More than just a fun drink to offer guests post-ceremony, the signature cocktail is a great way to share your tastes with your guests. Is there a drink you and your S.O. always mix up on Friday nights? Spend your engagement perfecting it, then have your bartenders recreate it on your wedding day. Does that bar down the street have a killer cocktail menu? Ask the bartender for the recipes for your usual orders.

A MOUTHWATERING MEAL

Who says your wedding dinner has to be steak, chicken, or fish? If there's a go-to meal you and your partner always share for special occasions, there's no occasion more special than your wedding day. Add a pasta course to the menu so you can feature that incredible dish you enjoyed on your trip to Italy, or offer an indulgent braised short rib (based on your own recipe) as the main course.

To keep these personal touches feeling fresh and refined rather than cheesy, exercise a bit of restraint, keeping the occasion in mind. Choose a few impactful personal touches that guests will really notice, then keep other details classic. Know what's appropriate for your wedding and what might be a better fit for the rehearsal dinner or another pre-wedding event. For example, your love of barbecue may not fit in with a black tie reception, but it could be perfect for the welcome party. Continue to make thoughtful and intentional choices throughout the planning process, and you'll be surprised by how personalized your wedding feels simply because you took the time to make decisions that felt right to the two of you.

WEDDING-READY PETS

Getting a fur-baby is what made you a family, so you can't leave your pet out of your wedding! If your venue is dog-friendly, have your pup walk down the aisle and sit with the two of you at the altar. If they're pet-free (or you've got cats or other pets that may not be quite so social), ask an illustrator to draw them so you can use that image on cocktail napkins or other signage. You could also use your pet's name as the title for your signature cocktail (Midge's Mai Tai, anyone?) or incorporate them into your cake topper or the groom's cake design.

PHOTOGRAPHY AND VIDEOGRAPHY

When your wedding day is over, you will have a heart full of memories and an album full of stunning photographs. But finding the right person to capture your big day requires more than just hiring a person with a camera. Find the right style—and the right professional—to preserve the details and candid moments of this milestone celebration.

CHOOSING A PHOTOGRAPHER

Choosing the perfect photographer begins with a lot of research. Pore over Instagram feeds, portfolios, and wedding magazines to find photos and photography styles you love, using these to identify the type of work that speaks to you. Do you prefer classic, posed portraits and composed shots; the movement and emotion of a photojournalistic style; or the softness of fine art photography? From there, look at local photographers' portfolios to find one who does similar work. Be sure to interview your potential photographer to make sure you get along personally, too. They're the one vendor you will spend the most time with, so you should seek out someone who makes you feel at ease. In addition to portfolios, ask to see a few full wedding albums from recent clients. This may mean looking over hundreds of images, but you'll get a sense of how the photographer captures each moment and whether they're looking for the details that matter to you, too.

FILM VS. DIGITAL PHOTOGRAPHY

While there are a myriad of photography styles out there, they fall into two main camps: film and digital. Cost and style can play a big role in which you choose (film photography is often more expensive due to the cost of film and processing, and each medium produces a different style of image), but there are other big factors to consider. Film photography, for example, is better at capturing detail even on a very sunny day (great for an outdoor wedding in the summer) while digital can be more effective in low light (such as at an indoor venue or during the later part of the evening). Film photography has an inherent feel of depth and softness, while digital photography can be edited to produce a photographer's signature final result (and can even closely replicate the look of film). As you talk to potential photographers, discuss the details of your event, your venue, and the types of images you are hoping for to determine which medium and which photographer will be the best fit.

AN ARGUMENT FOR VIDEOGRAPHY

Often the last thing added to a wedding budget, today's wedding videography is a far cry from the wedding films of yore. Hiring a videographer may be a splurge, but the extra investment is worth it when you consider the returns. Nothing captures emotion quite like video. You can relive the moment of your first kiss, your flower girl's spin around the dance floor, or smiles of your loved ones in a way that photography can't replicate. You can witness the moments you may have missed while you were standing at the altar or busy having your dress bustled, and you can hear the sounds of your partner reading his or her vows or your guests laughing at the toasts again and again. Wedding videography is a unique way to capture and save the living moments of your wedding day that you wouldn't be able to otherwise, all in a package that can be shared and savored for years to come.

AN "UNPLUGGED" CEREMONY

To get the most from your professional photography, consider asking guests to silence and put away their phones and personal cameras during the ceremony. While it's great to collect candid photos from guests during the reception, you don't want your photographer's view obstructed by outstretched arms holding cameras as you walk down the aisle, nor do you want the video footage of your vows interrupted by a ringing phone. A simple sign at the entrance to your venue or a note in the program is a polite way to make this request, or you may have your officiant make an annoucement before the processional begins.

TABLESIDE POLAROIDS Expand your photo collection from the big day by asking your guests to be photographers, too. Place cameras throughout the reception venue, and invite everyone to take photos of anything they'd like throughout the celebration. You'll wind up with a diverse collection of images, capturing all those moments your professional photographer couldn't catch.

SELECTING YOUR FLOWERS

Weddings and flowers go together like you and your partner. These highly visible décor elements range from personal accessories to statement-making installations at the reception, and no other detail will appear quite so much throughout your celebration. But with a great florist and a clear vision in mind, a floral design that takes your wedding style to the next level is within reach.

HOW TO PICK A FLORIST WHO GETS YOUR STYLE

Flowers make up a significant portion of your wedding décor, and finding a florist who understands your style and can execute your vision is a tall order. As you're looking at potential florists, spend time reviewing their portfolios to get a feel for the type of work they create. Read reviews for an insight into past couples' experiences. When you meet in person, don't be afraid to ask questions. Come prepared with an explanation of the style you're seeking, and listen closely as the florist responds. If she or he gets excited about your ideas—and shares a few new ideas that you totally love—you've found your florist.

HOW TO TRANSLATE YOUR STYLE INTO FLOWERS

LAVISH

Fill a lavish wedding with lush and dramatic flowers as far as the eye can see. Pair ornate arrangements with luxe accents, like sparkling crystal or polished metallics. If you're designing on a budget, focus on a single statement-making detail, like a spectacular head table or an incredible overhead arrangement above the dance floor.

RUSTIC

Create an organic ambiance for a rustic wedding by opting for soft arrangements with hand-gathered appeal. Mix in greenery, natural elements like feathers, and berries for texture. Continue the organic feeling in the vessels you choose, with blooms spilling out of wooden boxes or perfectly weathered ceramics.

ROMANTIC

For a romantic wedding, create a living fairy tale with soft flowers in feminine arrangements. Polished silver and clear glass are both at home on your tables, surrounded by trailing greenery and candlelight. Emphasize romantic accents like silk ribbons and touches of lace.

MODERN

Modern weddings are all about sleek and structural details. Monochromatic—and even single-varietal—arrangements will set your floral design apart. Opt for blooms with crisp shapes, like calla lilies or tulips, to mirror the clean lines you have created elsewhere with your design, and select streamlined vases to match.

ELEGANT

Choose timeless, polished floral design for an elegant wedding. Manicured arrangements, with every bloom placed just so, are classics for a reason! Ask your florist to use traditional vessels in a finish that matches your palette, and don't forget the votive candles.

VINTAGE

When designing a vintage wedding, keep your time period and palette in mind. Look for flowers with a soft, time-worn feel, mixing in dusty miller and baby's breath for a retro finish. If the Art Deco era is your inspiration, a trailing presentation bouquet—whether of sculptural calla lilies or a dramatic combination of blooms and greenery—will tuck neatly into the crook of your arm.

POPULAR FLOWERS BY STYLE

Some flowers have a more distinct style than others, making them a winning choice if you are not sure where to start when it comes to your floral design. These are some of the most popular blooms to choose, based on your wedding style.

LAVISH: PEONIES

Peonies are luxe and dramatic—perfect for a lavish wedding. These full and soft blooms come in a wide range of colors and make a major statement however they're used.

RUSTIC: RANUNCULUS

Rustic weddings are just the place to use ranunculus. The tightly packed petals look like a smaller, more relaxed version of a peony or garden rose, comfortable tucked into an organic bouquet and a boutonniere.

ROMANTIC: GARDEN ROSES

Nothing says "romantic wedding" quite like a garden rose. The full and fluffy hybrid of a traditional rose, garden roses are soft and sweet with feminine, fairy tale appeal.

MODERN: TULIPS

The sculptural shape of a tulip is ideal for a modern wedding. Crisp and classy, these cheerful flowers can be gathered into large bunches for maximum visual impact. Ranging from pure white to bold and bright, they'll fit any color scheme.

ELEGANT: ROSES

Roses and weddings are a classic pairing, ideal for an elegant celebration. Use a single color for a little more drama, or combine a few shades and varieties for soft texture.

VINTAGE: HYDRANGEAS

Fill your vintage wedding with huge, soft arrangements of hydrangeas. These blooms, with multi-toned petals that appear softened with time, give you bang for your buck and have a decidedly Old World vibe.

WHAT TO CONSIDER WHEN SELECTING FLOWERS

As you're deciding which flowers you'll use at your wedding and how you'll arrange them, take time to consider where your flowers are coming from. Talk to your florist about how flowers are sourced and what's in season to get the look you've dreamed of and make the most of your budget.

LOCALLY GROWN FLOWERS

There are so many reasons to go local. Just like produce in the grocery store, locally grown flowers are in-season, support local businesses, and will give your wedding a sense of place. Locally grown flowers are also more sustainable, as they don't have to be loaded into refrigerated airplanes and flown halfway around the world. But of course, it all comes down to looks. The benefit of local flowers is that they are blooms that thrive nearby—which means you will get a different selection if you're marrying in Georgia or California. Yes, some flowers are grown just about everywhere, but it's those local ones that will say "this is where you got married" when you look at the photos.

IMPORTED FLOWERS

Got your heart set on peonies but you're getting married in October? Well, there's a pretty good chance those flowers will be imported. After all, Fall in North America means Spring in South America, so the floral seasons will be flip-flopped. Some countries, such as the Netherlands and Colombia, have massive floral export businesses, which means even those in-season flowers may be coming from somewhere else. The benefit of using imported blooms (whether from another country or simply shipped from a different part of the U.S.) is that you can get your dream flowers year-round, making those blooming seasons feel much longer than they actually are.

THE BENEFITS OF DESIGNING SEASONALLY

While you can get just about any flower at nearly any time of year, filling your centerpieces and bouquets with out-of-season flowers will greatly increase the cost, as the blooms will have to be imported from across the globe or carefully cultivated in pricey greenhouses. A fantastic way to keep your flower budget in check and give your wedding a sense of time and place is to opt, instead, for in-season blooms. After all, Mother Nature knows what she's doing!

SPRING

In the spring, look for blossoming branches like cherry blossoms and dogwood, as well as fragrant lily of the valley. Tulips and sweet peas will also begin to bloom, as will some ranunculus and roses, depending on your region. Brides marrying in late spring and early summer will be happy to find peonies aplenty at the flower market.

SUMMER

Garden roses and hydrangeas are in full bloom through the summer, filling out centerpieces and bouquets. Other playful blooms, such as cosmos and clematis, add texture to arrangements, while delphiniums are a must-have for classic summer brides.

FALL

Dahlia lovers will have the best selection to choose from in fall months, whether petite pompons or dramatic dinnerplates. Hydrangeas continue to bloom in the fall, as do cosmos. Chrysanthemums and gerbera daisies are a textured seasonal alternative to dahlias, and can pack a punch of color.

WINTER

Fewer flowers bloom in the winter (unless you are in a warm, snow-free region), which makes greenery and ornamental berries go-to options to fill out winter arrangements. Evergreen and eucalyptus—alongside viburnum, brunia, and tallow berries—pair perfectly with select greenhouse or imported blooms.

"Nature is full of inspiration. Consider the color and shape of every bloom—and even the leaves—to create a stunning composition."

spring

summer

fall

winter

NONFLORAL OPTIONS

When most people think of wedding decorations, they jump straight to flowers, but those aren't the only items you can use to deck out your tables or cover your altar. Greenery, grasses, branches, and berries add texture and volume—and can even replace those flowers.

GREENERY

Greenery is more than just filler. Rustic and romantic brides love eucalyptus, whether the seeded or silver dollar variety, for its muted green color and subtle scent. Elegant brides often turn to ruscus, a more traditional greenery that still adds volume. And don't forget the soft, pale green that comes with dusty miller! If you're having a tropical wedding, large palm or monstera leaves can create huge three-dimensional arrangements or serve as natural chargers on the table. Should you wish to skip flowers altogether, but want something with a floral shape, succulents can give your design a textural finish (plus they make great wedding favors!).

GRASSES

Grasses are a beautiful way to add height and fullness to your floral design, and can even replace flowers altogether for a more rustic and relaxed finish. Pampas grass is one of the most popular options. Dried pampas has a flowing shape and beige color that's a perfect neutral, topped with a bushy plume. For a grass that packs more of a green punch (but that same soft texture), look to explosion grass. The wispy top looks like a glowing sparkler, eye-catching as a filler or on its own. Other more traditional grasses, such as lily grass and bear grass, are long and sleek with a vivid green color.

BRANCHES AND LEAVES

Cherry blossoms aren't the only branches you'll see at weddings. Olive branches are a favorite of romantic and vintage brides, with two-toned leaves that add lots of depth. More classic brides prefer the deep green color of magnolia leaves, with a rich copper tone on the back. Aspen and birch branches create beautifully organic arches and altars, whether draped with flowers or left bare. Long, curly willow branches add airy height, while the more solid branches of manzanita trees are surprisingly modern.

BERRIES

Add more texture to your arrangements with berries. No matter the color of your blooms, you'll be able to find the perfect hypericum berry to fit your palette. From white and green to blush, pink, peach, coral and even deep red, pick a color that will pop against the rest of your bouquet. Silver brunia is a silver-gray textured berry on a textured green stem, a must-have to add depth to white flowers. Or add a bit of drama with deep blue privet berries, which are surprisingly versatile (and look incredible paired with olive leaves in a boutonniere).

ALTERNATIVES TO POPULAR FLOWERS

Peonies and dahlias may be all the rage, but whether they're out of season or out of budget, filling your bouquets with trendy flowers isn't always possible. These six blooms top brides' must-have lists—and have dupes so beautiful, you'll barely notice the difference.

HYDRANGEAS ⋙ STOCK FLOWERS

It's hard to match the volume of hydrangeas, so focus instead on the delicate petals. Stock flowers have a similar shape (at a much lower cost), and come in a comparable range of hues. Trim back the greenery and cluster stems together for a full, lush look.

STEPHANOTIS ⋙ FREESIA

This flowering vine has star-shaped flowers and an unmistakable scent, but the delicate blooms come with a high price. Instead, use freesia, which is slightly more full but also much easier to come by!

PEONIES ⋙ GARDEN ROSES

The layered petals and fluffy interior of a peony is hard to duplicate, but garden roses come close. While these flowers aren't always more affordable than peonies, they do have a longer season, making garden roses much easier to find.

DAHLIAS ⋙ CHRYSANTHEMUMS

When swapping in chrysanthemums for dahlias, it's all about finding a variety that has a sharp, clean shape. Reflex chrysanthemums have curved petals that, as they begin to open, mimic the shape of a dahlia, while a football mum has a large, full shape somewhere between a dahlia and a peony.

LILY OF THE VALLEY ⋙ WHITE PIERIS

These delicate, bell-shaped flowers have a sweet and memorable scent, but can be out of many brides' price range. For a similar look, ask instead for white pieris. Another bell-shaped bloom, the cascading flowers are clustered more densely than lily of the valley, and Pieris is also available in shades of pink.

SWEET PEA ⋙ BOUGAINVILLEA

Sweet peas are a climbing flower with soft, ruffled petals. They are most available in the springtime, a challenge for summer brides who love the delicate appearance. Bougainvillea is acclimated to warmer weather, meaning these equally delicate and colorful blooms are a beautiful alternative.

PERFECT PERSONAL FLOWERS

Make your dresses and suits stand out with the perfect floral accessories. Get to know your choices, then customize your bouquets and boutonnieres to make each arrangement your own.

BOUQUET SHAPES

In addition to the flowers you select, the shape of your bouquet will play a role in enhancing your wedding style. From small and sweet to organic and sprawling, there are so many shapes and styles to choose from—but these are the most common options.

POSEY

A petite bouquet often created for bridesmaids or flower girls, a posey features a few flowers, subtle greenery, and a wrapped stem that is easy to hold in one hand.

NOSEGAY

Slightly larger than a posey, a nosegay features more greenery and a few more blooms for volume. This is another popular bridesmaid choice, as well as a lovely option for petite brides.

ROUND

These iconic mid-sized bouquets are heavy on the flowers, with a few varieties paired with little to no greenery. The flowers are arranged tightly to give the bouquet its structured shape.

CASCADE

A dramatic floral statement, cascade bouquets trail over the hands and down the front of the dress, usually with blooming vines or greenery draping to create the teardrop shape.

PRESENTATION

Also called a pageant bouquet, this style is designed to be held in one arm, with the flowers resting in the crook of your elbow. Calla lilies, orchids, and other long-stemmed blooms are most common for this modern style, though a softer and more romantic look can be created with other flowers and grasses.

HAND-TIED

Hand-tied bouquets are designed to look as though the flowers have been gathered during a walk in the garden, softly tied with ribbon. This rustic, romantic look is looser and finished with a ribbon tie.

CRESCENT

Large, sprawling bouquets—a lush interpretation of a hand-tied style—are incredibly popular, and often take on a crescent shape that arcs across the front of the body. Flowers are concentrated in the center, tapering off to the sides with the addition of longer stems or greenery. These can be kept classic and symmetrical, or made asymmetrical for a more romantic and organic feel.

BOUTONNIERE BASICS

These small but mighty floral arrangements, pinned to a man's left lapel right over the heart, add a dressed up final touch to menswear that ties in with women's bouquets and other floral accessories. Worn by the groom, groomsmen, ring bearers, the couple's fathers and brothers, and often the officiant, it also signifies who is a VIP in a sea of men in suits. There's more to boutonnieres than simply sticking a flower into a buttonhole, so here's how to pick a design that lasts all day.

SIZE MATTERS

The size of a boutonniere should be scaled so it fits comfortably on the lapel and doesn't overwhelm the wearer. Men's boutonnieres should be slightly larger than those for boys, between three and four inches long for men and two and three inches for boys. Anything much larger can be top heavy and tip over instead of staying at a jaunty angle.

CHOOSE STURDY BLOOMS

Boutonnieres are out of water for much longer than bouquets, meaning the elements you choose need to be sturdy. Orchids, roses, ranunculus, and even hellebores are all hardy blooms that can last. Anemones, smoke bush, and hydrangea blossoms are quite delicate and will show lack of water quickly.

INCLUDE NONFLORAL ACCENTS

A single flower can make for a striking boutonniere, but most benefit from a nonfloral accent to make the bloom pop. Fresh herbs like rosemary are fragrant and structural, while a few olive or eucalyptus leaves are a pretty backdrop. Tufts of dried grasses or curling ferns can add texture, as can elements like feathers or seed pods.

ORDER A BACK-UP

With all the hugging you'll be doing, your boutonniere may look a little worse for wear after cocktail hour. If you're worried about its appearance, ask your florist to include a second boutonniere for the groom that can be swapped out before you make your grand entrance into the reception.

CALLA LILY Make a bold statement with a single, sculptural bloom like the calla lily. The white petals stand out against a dark tux, and its clean, simple lines are perfect for a modern wedding. It's a sturdy flower that will last all day.

FINISHING TOUCHES

You've chosen the flowers and shape of your bouquet and selected a coordinating boutonniere, so now it's time to tie it all together, literally, with a few finishing touches. Who knew there were so many choices for what you can use to wrap your bouquet?

RIBBONS AND WRAPS

While wire and floral tape are what really hold bouquets and boutonnieres together, they're not very photogenic, which is why florists wrap the stems for a clean final look. A satin ribbon is a classic option, and it comes in every color of the rainbow. If you'd like a bouquet with a more romantic vibe, hand-dyed silk ribbons have become incredibly popular—and many brides opt to leave trailing lengths of ribbon that will catch the breeze during an outdoor ceremony. For a masculine finish on a boutonniere, use suede or leather to wrap the stem. Woven cord can add a pop of color, a touch of twine is recognizably rustic, and a velvet ribbon (on either a boutonniere or a bouquet) is elegant and luxe.

ACCESSORIES

To dress up your bouquet even further, replace standard floral pins with a crystal-topped variety for a touch of sparkle. More ornate wraps can also give your stems some personality, whether embroidered with your monogram or featuring beautiful beadwork.

FAMILY HEIRLOOMS

You may have a few of your nearest and dearest offering you family heirlooms to incorporate into your big day. Adding these heirlooms to your bouquet is a beautiful way to keep loved ones with you as you make your way down the aisle. Wrap your bouquet with a piece of your mother's wedding dress or your great-grandmother's handkerchief. A rosary or other necklace can also be pinned around the stems. If you have other pieces of jewelry, such as a ring, that you want to carry but don't want to wear, have your florist tie a ribbon to the piece that can then be secured to your bouquet with pins. Don't forget to remove any heirloom pieces before tucking your bouquet back into water after the ceremony!

FLORAL DÉCOR

Weddings are nearly synonymous with flowers, a lush and fragrant way to transform a space and add color and texture to the celebration. Whether you want to make a dramatic statement with flowers everywhere they'll fit, or envision a more modern design with sleek and sparse blooms, there are a number of places you'll most likely see flowers pop up—and endless options for how each piece will look.

CEREMONY FLOWERS

In addition to the bouquets and boutonnieres, flowers make an appearance in a few key places at the ceremony, which will serve to enhance—or totally transform—your venue.

THE ALTAR

Whether it's the altar of a house of worship, a towering fireplace, or a stunning natural arch on a sprawling lawn, the altar will frame you and your spouse as you exchange vows. In a house of worship, a garland of greenery and blooms could be draped across a table, or two arrangements in ceramic urns could flank you and your officiant. For an outdoor wedding, choose an arch that fits your style (whether it's sleek copper, rustic birch branches, or a quaint pergola), then dress it how you see fit, using blooms that coordinate with your bouquet and match your color palette. Add extra drama by putting coordinating arrangements (or even another arch!) at the head of the aisle, too.

THE AISLE

Set the scene for your grand entrance with a gorgeous aisle. Tie petite posies to the ends of each pew, or edge the aisle in low floral arrangements surrounded by pillar candles in metal lanterns. Make a more rustic statement with a border of pampas grass and lupines or lavender. Pillowy petals (or seasonal elements like red and orange leaves for a fall wedding) also make exceptional aisle borders.

COCKTAIL HOUR ACCENTS

Cocktail hour flowers are often overlooked, but these small arrangements can be big on style. Use this as an opportunity to transition from your ceremony design to the palette and design accents guests will see once they arrive at the ceremony—and don't forget the bar.

BUD VASES

Cocktail tables are small, which means bud vases are your friend when it comes to adding a few flowers. Look for vases that fit your style, whether they're simple glass, modern metallic, or sleek ceramic. A bloom or two and some greenery will still pack a punch, especially when paired with votive candles—and this smaller selection will leave plenty of space for guests to set down their drinks.

BAR ACCENTS

Cocktail hour gets its name from the drinks, so don't forget to dress up the bar! Keep the design simple by using a few of those bud vase arrangements, clustered together in the corner of the bar next to the cocktail menu. For more of a statement, edge the bar in one oversize arrangement that will definitely get guests' attention. (This is a great place to repurpose bridesmaids' bouquets, as well.) If you want the drinks to be the focal point, drape a garland across the front of the bar to soften the set-up without distracting.

RECEPTION

It's time for the main event! As you're putting together a plan for the reception flowers, think about the feeling you want to create for your guests. Use flowers, candles, and other nonfloral accents to transport them to a magical world that's all about celebrating your love.

CENTERPIECE SHAPES AND STYLES

Work closely with your florist to create centerpieces that match your wedding style and tie into your color palette. Look for vessels and arrangements of blooms that help enhance your theme, coordinating each piece with the rest of your design. Keep height, density, and budget in mind as you're making your choices to come up with an immersive design scheme.

BUD VASE CLUSTERS

For a delicate effect, cluster bud vases of varying heights across the table. Combine different flowers and greenery for a gathered look, or limit each vase for a single variety (or a single bloom, like one overblown peony) for a more modern take. Mix in votive and taper candles to bring height to the table.

LOW BOWLS AND URNS

The most classic option for centerpieces, these vessels give you much more real estate to work with, whether you're envisioning something tight and manicured or sprawling and romantic. Elegant brides love cut crystal and silver compotes, vintage brides are drawn to mercury glass, and rustic brides adore concrete or terracotta urns.

TALL AND ELEVATED ARRANGEMENTS

In a venue with high ceilings or for a more dramatic setting, mix in tall vases and elevated arrangements to add height to your design. Group sculptural blooms, such as branches of delphinium or fluffy hydrangeas, in narrow vases. Give other tables a romantic finish by perching arrangements atop metal stands or between the arms of a candelabra.

GARLANDS

Keep centerpieces low by getting rid of the vessels altogether, instead laying garlands down the center of each table. For an elegant wedding, stud a garland of magnolia leaves or eucalyptus with garden roses and lisianthus. Or go lavish with a garland made entirely of flowers for a fragrant and eye-catching statement. Whatever you choose, weave the garland between candles in coordinating holders to cast a warm glow over the table.

OVERHEAD ARRANGEMENTS

This floral installation tops many a bride's wish list. Overhead arrangements of flowers and greenery bring your wedding design to new heights. Drape an existing chandelier with smilax or eucalyptus, or ask your florist to create a stunning display of inverted blooms dangling dramatically over the dance floor. If you opt to go up with your floral décor, keep the designs on the tables simple so that statement piece really pops.

NONFLORAL ACCENTS

The addition of nonfloral accents gives centerpieces depth and visual interest, and can help create a lived-in feel. Scatter bowls of fresh fruit between the flowers, or turn to on-theme objects like geodes, antlers, delicate ceramics, or even driftwood and coral. If all you want is romance, skip the flowers altogether and cover your tables with as many candles as you can fit. Vary the heights of the candles but keep the votive holders and candlesticks in a cohesive palette for a streamlined and striking effect.

FINISHING TOUCHES

Take the flowers out of the centerpieces for a delicate finish to your reception design. Give each place setting a pretty finishing touch by tucking a bloom into each napkin, or placing a sprig of herbs atop a printed menu. Make the seats of honor stand out with garlands of flowers and greenery, or tuck a few blooms into chair signs flaunting your newlywed status.

REUSE ARRANGEMENTS TO STRETCH YOUR BUDGET

The urge to put flowers on every surface can add up quickly, and you may find the statement you want to make is out of your budget. Instead of splurging on new arrangements for every moment of your wedding day, work with your florist to wisely repurpose blooms. Aisle markers tied to chairs or pews can be tucked into bud vases and set on cocktail tables, and altar arrangements can be moved to flank the door to the reception or decorate the corners of the stage. Many florists will also rent additional vases to hold the bridal and bridesmaids bouquets and transform them into centerpieces, whether they're scattered amongst candles on the head table or used to dress up the bar and the cake table. Having a brunch the next morning? Ask your florist for a quote to store your centerpieces and reuse them on the breakfast tables—which will still be much less than ordering brand new arrangements.

DONATE YOUR FLOWERS
The hardest thing about spending money on wedding flowers is knowing they'll be thrown away at the end of the night—but they don't have to be. Talk to your florist, planner, or venue about options for donating your centerpieces once your wedding has come to an end. They will be able to suggest organizations that facilitate giving your blooms to hospitals and retirement homes, helping brighten up someone else's day with a dose of the love that shone on yours.

PLANNING YOUR CEREMONY

If there is one thing that makes a wedding more than just a party, it's the ceremony. It's an opportunity for you and your partner to make promises to one another, surrounded by the people you love most. Instead of leaving the details to the last minute, prioritize your ceremony (and the marriage you'll build together) and transform it into something truly memorable. Sit down with your future spouse, think about how you want that moment to look and feel, and prepare to write the next chapter in your love story.

DETERMINING YOUR CEREMONY STYLE

Wedding ceremonies come in all shapes and sizes, from elaborate and traditional to short and heartfelt. Before you think about the flowers or the music, you and your partner will need to determine what type of ceremony you'd like to have, as this can impact where and how you tie the knot.

RELIGIOUS CEREMONIES

If you and your partner would like to have a religious ceremony, begin by speaking to a religious leader who you'd like to have officiate. He or she will be able to guide you through any religious requirements as you determine what type of ceremony you will be able to have. Some denominations can easily have religious ceremonies at nonreligious venues, while others require that the ceremony be performed in a house of worship. Understanding these requirements early will make all of the following details much easier to manage.

CIVIL CEREMONIES

Presided over by a legal official (such as a judge, justice of the peace, mayor, or county clerk), these ceremonies are regulated only by your local county or state's legal marriage regulations. They can occur anywhere—provided your chosen officiant is willing to come and preside over the proceedings—and the content can be customized and personalized much further than a religious ceremony.

OTHER LEGAL CEREMONIES

Have you always dreamed of having a close friend or family member officiate? This popular alternative makes a ceremony even more personal by having someone you know and love take on the task of telling your love story. Every aspect of this ceremony can be made your own, whether you ask your officiant to surprise you with his or her words, or you work with them to draft a ceremony that perfectly encapsulates your relationship. Just be sure to check any local requirements to ensure your ceremony is legally recognized.

CHOOSING A CEREMONY VENUE

Once you determine the style of ceremony you'd like to have, select a venue that fits both your ceremony and your wedding style. If you are having a religious ceremony, you may wish to wed in a house of worship. These venues can be simple or elaborate, but the priority is to choose one with a religious leader who you feel best represents the promises you and your partner are preparing to make.

For a nonreligious ceremony, there are still a number of options to consider. The most popular is to have your ceremony on-site at your reception venue, whether it is at an outdoor space or another indoor area. Keep the weather and the size of your guest list in mind to

ensure everyone will be comfortable—and don't forget to discuss a rain plan with your venue if you're eyeing an outdoor ceremony.

Some couples also opt to have their ceremony at a different venue altogether, especially if their reception venue can't accommodate both a ceremony and a reception. Look at nearby event spaces and public spaces that are available for rent, such as the dramatic lobby of a metropolitan City Hall. Factor transportation time between each venue into your timeline, allowing guests to get from place to place, and consider offering a shuttle to make arriving at the reception even easier.

DECORATING YOUR CEREMONY SPACE

Your ceremony is the introduction to your day of celebration. As you consider how you would like to decorate your venue, choose colors and elements that tie into your overall design scheme, creating a progression from the moment the ceremony begins to the night's very last dance.

Because ceremonies often take place earlier in the day, a more muted version of your palette will softly announce the design to come.

Display flowers in the same style you've chosen for the reception, whether soft and organic or manicured and precise. Keep fonts consistent across your invitations, ceremony programs, and reception paper goods. Weave in other highlighted design elements, such as pops of metallics or natural elements like wood, antlers, or feathers—guests will spot them at the ceremony and notice them again once they've arrived at cocktail hour.

NONTRADITIONAL CEREMONY SET-UPS

Most ceremony set-ups follow a similar pattern, no matter the venue: rows of chairs flank an aisle, which leads to an altar marked by an arch or floral arrangements. However, that isn't the only way to create a ceremony space.

UNIQUE STRUCTURES

If you love the idea of an arch as a focal point, but want to play with shape, consider other structures that can give you that "altar" feel in a creative way. Round or hexagonal metal structures can suspend flowers in an eye-catching shape. The poles of a teepee, left bare instead of draped in canvas, will frame a ceremony but still let nature in. And the imposing structure of a stone fireplace, softened with candles and flowers, creates a cozy backdrop for winter vows.

EXCITING ALTERNATIVES

Looking for something out of the box? Skip that altar shape altogether. Surround yourselves with beauty and love with a semicircle arrangement of flowers and grasses set on the ground surrounding the two of you. Or go romantic with dozens of oversized lanterns filled with glowing candlelight. If you're marrying outdoors at a venue with gorgeous trees, let them stand in as your arch, draping the branches in fabric and blooms. Or let nature speak for itself with a small rug or platform marking where you'll stand and only the beauty of your surroundings behind you.

CREATIVE SEATING ARRANGEMENTS

Rows of matching chairs aren't your only options. Swap the straight lines for a ceremony in the round, with either semicircles or circles of chairs surrounding the altar so you and your partner are literally surrounded by love. For a ceremony with a relaxed and welcoming feel, replace some of the chairs with rented sofas or other lounge furniture. If you adore the drama of a classic cathedral, but love the feel of the sunshine on your face, rent vintage church pews and arrange them in a spectacular natural setting.

WRITING YOUR CEREMONY

As you prepare to enter into this new era of your love story, it's time to choose the words that will set it all in motion. The stories you share and the vows you exchange are the things that make your wedding day momentous, and personalizing these elements will make your ceremony a reflection of who the two of you are as a couple. Pick and choose the aspects that tell your unique story, and there won't be a dry eye in the house.

INCORPORATING TRADITION

Traditions help us mark occasions, signifying that they have deeper meaning and connecting us with both the past and the future. The addition of traditions and rituals to a wedding ceremony will also help connect you to your guests, many of whom have followed those same traditions in their own lives. While many traditions are religious in nature, some (such as readings or songs, rituals like handfasting, or the lighting of candles) can be reinterpreted and woven into nonreligious ceremonies, should you so choose. Remember to look to cultural traditions, as well, as many of these cross religious boundaries with ease.

TELLING YOUR LOVE STORY

Your wedding is a major milestone in your relationship, and the content of your ceremony should reflect that. Work closely with your officiant to add the details of your love story to your ceremony. Discuss how you met and why you fell in love. Share the dreams you have for your future and the life you want to build together. Whether it is a religious ceremony or a secular one, these details will provide context for the promise you'll make to one another, as well as give your guests a peek into your romance.

WRITING YOUR VOWS

There is something so special about sharing words that have been observed by generations before us, and the appeal of traditional vows is not lost on many couples. Even those who choose to write their own vows often opt to incorporate aspects of traditional phrasing into the words they exchange. Though you and your partner may choose to write your vows separately and surprise one another on your wedding day, establish a general format so your vows fit together. In addition to sharing some of the highlights and challenges of your relationship (hey, nobody is perfect), agree on how many promises you'll each make to one another. You may even want to phrase them in a similar way, or alternate promises you write together with ones you write privately. Then, before you head down the aisle, spend time reading them out loud to make sure you're comfortable with the wording—and have some tissues handy!

WORDS OF LOVE Before you walk down the aisle, hand off your vows to a bridesmaid to hold until you need them. If you are going through the effort of writing your own vows, read them from something that fits your wedding style, like an elegant deckle-edged paper (not the yellow sticky notes you drafted them on).

CELEBRATING IN STYLE

It's time to celebrate! While the ceremony may be the most meaningful moment of your wedding day, the reception is the most anticipated—so let's make it a good one! As you start thinking about the details, be sure to cater to all of your guests' senses. The visual may come first, but as you get deeper into the design, think about how the flowers might smell, how the napkins or seat cushions will feel, what the music will sound like, and how the meal will taste, to create a layered experience that becomes immersive. Prioritize the details that are most important to you, whether it's a restaurant-quality meal or the most beautiful flowers your guests have ever seen, and you'll wind up with a personalized celebration that you'll remember forever.

DESIGNING YOUR TABLES

Setting a beautiful table won't just enhance the look of your reception. It will bring people together, helping to create a feeling of welcoming and hospitality that makes an event truly memorable. Whether you can invest in an opulent design, or are celebrating on a smaller budget and need to use it wisely, the intention of creating a beautiful presentation and consciously choosing items will shine through.

LINENS

As the base of your table design, choosing the right linen is like selecting a canvas. Floor-length linens give your reception an extra feeling of elegance, even in simple white. If you'd prefer a colored linen, choose one of the lighter tones in your palette (or a pastel version of your base color). This will allow you to layer in elements atop the linens without the rest of your details disappearing. There are also many options for printed and textured linens that can make your style feel more playful, especially when paired with solid colors or used to highlight the head or cake table. And don't forget the napkins! You could match napkins to the tablecloth, or choose a contrasting color or pattern to make each place setting pop.

PLACE SETTINGS

Place settings include four key ingredients: a charger, plates, glassware, and flatware. While traditional options feature white china, classic silverware, and simple glassware, you can mix in other colors and textures to further your wedding style. A unique charger, whether in a colorful print or an organic material such as slate, creates a backdrop upon which you can layer pieces you love. Flatware in gold or copper adds an elegant or modern touch, while wood-handled designs are romantic and rustic. And don't forget glassware—upgrade to more delicate crystal for a luxe, formal look, or turn to colored vintage glassware that perfectly matches your palette.

CENTERPIECES

No matter what your centerpieces are made of, make sure your guests will be able to see and talk to one another, either over or under the design. A few taller candles here and there won't get in anyone's way, but if all the flowers are at eye-level, they won't be able to see anyone on the other side of the table. Make sure you leave room for each place setting, as well as accoutrements like salt and pepper shakers or bread and butter trays.

PAPER GOODS

Take inspiration from your invitation suite when creating your reception paper goods. Pick place and escort cards, menus, and signage with similar colors and matching fonts for a feeling of continuity and well-informed guests. To make guests feel extra welcome, use menus personalized with their names as the place cards, or top each napkin with a hand-written note thanking them for being there with you to celebrate.

FURNITURE AND RENTALS

While flowers, linens, and dishes will help create an ambiance while guests are seated at the table, larger rental items will help transform a blank venue into an exciting and celebratory space. From the basics, including dinner tables and chairs, to design-focused pieces like stylized lounge furniture, rentals are the items that can really take your wedding style to new heights.

TABLES AND CHAIRS

Many venues include tables and chairs in their rental fee, but those no-fuss items aren't your only choices. Tables come in all different shapes and sizes, so you can pick and choose what fits your crowd. If you're not into linens, look at antique farm tables or other options that can be used bare or with runners. Line up king's tables end-to-end to create a long, dramatic banquet table that can seat every one of your guests. And don't forget the chairs—from rustic cross-backs to elegant Chivari, modern Lucite options to tropical cane, renting dinner chairs gives your design a polished finishing touch.

BARS

Bars don't have to be basic. Serve drinks in style at a rented bar that blends seamlessly with the rest of your design. Bars can be covered with elegant paneling, reclaimed wood planks, or even finished with custom panels featuring a pattern or your monogram. More modern styles can be customized with wraps specially chosen for your celebration. The bar back, a table set behind the bar where bartenders store glassware and bottles, can be upgraded with unique shelving (and then decorated with flowers or candles) to make your bar look like it's straight out of your favorite restaurant.

LOUNGE AREAS

If you've got extra room, look to additional rentals that can help give your venue a welcoming, lived-in feel that will make guests instantly relaxed. Furniture like sofas, arm chairs, and coffee tables add a residential touch that will make cocktail hour cozy or provide a stylish place for guests to take a break from the dance floor.

ACCENT PIECES

Little extras that go beyond florals put a finishing touch on your design. Soften those sofas with rented coordinating pillows (or custom cushions with your new monogram), toss throws over the backs of chairs, and top side or coffee tables with pieces like lamps, lanterns, or other artistic objects.

SEATING ARRANGEMENTS

Yes, escort and place cards have practical value, ensuring everyone has a seat and helping your caterer get the right meals to each table. But they also serve an emotional purpose—they don't just tell your guests where to sit, they announce that each guest has a place at your table, and that you've taken the time to seat them with people you think they'll enjoy. Match up guests with similar interests or backgrounds, or pair people who you think will find each other intriguing. A wedding is a great place to meet someone interesting or learn something new.

BON APPETIT!

Wedding meals often get a bad rap for being boring and bland, but they don't have to be. Even if you're working off a pre-set menu with standard options, you can make choices that will elevate the meal to something special. Impeccable service, a signature cocktail, and ample hors d'oeuvres can make your celebration shine. Most importantly, don't leave your guests hungry or waiting for a drink!

SERVICE STYLES

How you serve a meal to your guests will impact the ambiance you are creating, whether it's casual and relaxed or incredibly formal. No matter what you choose, select beautiful serveware to help elevate the meal. We eat with our eyes first, which is why coleslaw in a cut crystal bowl and barbecue on silver platters just tastes better!

BUFFET

Buffets are a more casual option, allowing guests to choose their own meal (and go back if they're still hungry!). It is also a fantastic alternative if you have a particularly large guest list where serving hundreds of guests tableside might be cost-prohibitive. Opt for a double-sided buffet or two buffet set-ups so the lines don't get too long, and employ the venue's staff to help you release tables so there isn't a mad rush for dinner.

STATIONS

A step up from a buffet (and more reminiscent of high-end buffet dining like you'd find in Las Vegas), a series of food stations allows you to offer a variety of options and encourage guests to explore different flavors. You could break up the stations by course (such as a salad station, a pasta station, and a carving station) or get creative with different cuisines (sushi, cheese and charcuterie, paella, or made-to-order Neapolitan pizzas). Stations can also be set up during cocktail hour as a form of entertainment, followed by a plated or family-style meal.

FAMILY-STYLE

Serving a meal family-style lets guests get comfortable at their seats and enjoy being served by your caterer's staff while still encouraging them to interact with one another and relax. Platters of food choices are set on the table, including a variety of proteins and sides, so guests can make their own plates and taste a little bit of everything. Consider beginning the meal with an individually plated salad or other appetizer before the main course is served. Family-style dining has even made its way into more formal celebrations, as it adds a touch of levity to what could otherwise be a stuffy evening.

PLATED MEAL

The most formal service option, a plated meal means each course is individually plated for guests and served to them at their seat. Plated meals usually require that you get guests' meal selections in advance via your RSVP card, though if you're in a restaurant-style setting your venue may offer a choice of meals at the table. To make this extra fancy, ask about French service—when each waiter carries a single plate and they serve an entire table in unison.

BEHIND THE BAR

Ask most wedding guests what they're most looking forward to, and the bar will rank at the top. There's nothing quite like raising a glass to mark a celebration, or a fantastic cocktail to get the conversation flowing and the dancing started, so give your bar some extra attention.

BEVERAGE SERVICE

Keep the drinks flowing and the lines short with a few easy beverage service tips. Avoid a traffic jam by having one bar (with two bartenders) for every 100 guests. Arrange multiple bars on opposite sides of the space to encourage guests to spread out. We've all been in that mad rush for a drink right after the ceremony, so consider tray-passing pre-poured drinks (such as glasses of bubbly, wine, or your signature cocktail) so guests can find a beverage without getting in line. Once it is time to eat, many guests will switch from cocktails to wine, so offer tableside wine service so they won't have to get up in search of a drink. And whatever you're serving, don't forget the water. Place a water station at the end of each bar so guests can skip the line and stay hydrated.

GLASSWARE

The right glassware will play easily into your wedding style, as well as make those drinks look oh-so-chic. A highball glass, a lowball glass, and red and white wine glasses will have you covered for just about everything. Serving beer on tap? Add pint glasses to the mix. Don't forget flutes for bubbly, or coupes if you're in more of a vintage mindset. To take your beverage service to the next level, explore upgraded glassware like delicate stemware for wine or a playful glass for your signature cocktail—think colored vintage glasses or even a tiki cup.

COCKTAILS

Everyone has "their drink," so a well-stocked bar will keep guests happy as they're sipping. Stock the basics (vodka, whiskey, tequila, and gin) along with mixers for easy pouring, and don't forget the garnishes. If you and your partner have particular tastes, upgrade to top shelf options or seek out unique bottles and blends guests may not have seen before. A fabulous signature cocktail, a few beers, and some delicious wine, and you're ready for a party.

BAR ON A BUDGET

Alcohol can get pricey in a hurry, but don't abandon ship in favor of a cash bar quite yet! Offer fewer, well-curated options to keep costs low while still making sure there's plenty of choices for everyone. Instead of a full bar, serve one or two signature cocktails plus wine and beer. Or limit the full bar to just cocktail hour, serving only beer and wine once dinner is served. For toasts, skip the pricey champagne and have guests raise whatever drink they've chosen for the night. If you must have champagne, opt for half pours instead of a full glass—most of your guests won't finish it, anyway.

GRANDMA KNOWS BEST

Even with a meal on the way, make sure there is something for guests to nibble on. Offer appetizers, whether passed or set out on trays, to ease the impact of alcohol during cocktail hour, and consider having a few bites preset on the table—such as a charcuterie board or bread and delicious spreads—to tide guests over during toasts (just like the snacks your grandmother always has ready the moment you arrive).

CAKES AND SWEETS

Couples cut wedding cake and feed one another a bite to symbolize a sweet beginning to their marriage. From spectacular cakes to your favorite sweets, pick the perfect dessert to ensure your marriage starts off on a delicious note, too.

CAKE DESIGN

Whether you'd like a simple cake topped with a few flowers or a dramatically carved or covered design that makes a major statement, the outside of a wedding cake is nearly as important as what's inside. As you're meeting with your baker, bring along your color palette and inspiration photos so she or he can get a sense of the style of your celebration. Even the details of your wedding dress can play a role in the final style. Loop in your florist if you'd like to add fresh flowers to the design, or wow your guests with incredible sugar work.

CHOOSING FLAVORS

Cake tasting might be the most fun part of planning a wedding. What could be more delicious than pairing cakes and frostings for that perfect bite? Classic flavors, like almond cake with vanilla frosting or white cake with fresh berries and cream, will never go out of style, but bakers today are getting creative with their offerings. Whether it's colorful funfetti, deep chocolate with peanut butter mousse, or a ribbon of delicious passion fruit curd, this is one dessert you'll never forget, so make it memorable! Let the season inspire your choices (fresh berries in the summer, warm spices in the winter), and know that you won't be able to please everyone, so have fun and pick a cake that you and your partner love.

ALTERNATIVE DESSERTS

Who says you have to serve cake at your wedding? If another sweet tickles your fancy, serve that as a mouthwatering ending to your wedding meal. From cookie tables and cupcake spreads to your favorite pies, the world of desserts is your oyster. Interactive displays are a creative way for guests to explore your favorite flavors, while a refined plated dessert like a mousse or individual tart is a chic end to a formal meal.

ENTERTAINMENT

Once everyone has eaten and the cake is cut, it's time to get the party started! Great entertainment will have your guests smiling and the dance floor packed, so dial up the energy and put on your dancing shoes.

BAND OR DJ?

Will your guests be dancing to a live band or the expert spinning of a DJ? A few factors come into play as you make your choice. First, consider what type of music you love. If you're fans of top 40 and wedding favorites, either option will work great for you. If you have very particular musical tastes, though, you'll either need a band in the same genre or may want a DJ who can play exactly what you're looking for. Do you love covers, or are you all about the original? A DJ is able to play a song the way the artist recorded it, while a band will put their own spin on the tune. Also consider how much space you will have at your venue. Smaller spaces often work better with DJs, as their equipment takes up much less room than is needed for even a small band. Worried about a cheesy DJ or band leader? Ask for reviews from recent clients, or see if you might be able to contact them yourselves. Someone who has used the service will be able to tell you how chatty the entertainer may be, helping you find a pro who fits your vision.

LAYERING LIVE MUSIC

You may want to offer multiple types of entertainment throughout the evening, such as an acoustic guitarist during the ceremony, a jazz trio during cocktail hour and dinner, and a larger band for dancing. If live music is your goal, look for a band that can offer it all—a single musician and singer early in the evening, then more and more band members until you reach the full band when it's time to party. This can often be much more affordable than hiring a few different ensembles for an hour each.

FORMAL DANCES

The first dance and dances with your parents are usually the last formality of the evening, and these few minutes on the dance floor turn into cherished memories. Take time to pick a song that holds meaning for you, whether it's one you've loved forever or a new tune with lyrics you love—and remember to read those lyrics to make sure you're on board with everything the song says! Whether you choose a sweet high school sway, a few fancy spins, or a fully choreographed number, embrace this time in the spotlight! If you don't love the attention, ask your band or DJ to cut each dance short, to about a minute and a half—this way you'll have plenty of time for pictures and happy tears, but won't be out of your comfort zone for too long.

ALTERNATIVE ENTERTAINMENT

Nondancers shouldn't be stuck in their seats all evening. If you know some of your crowd won't be on the dance floor, offer alternative entertainment to keep them engaged all evening. Arrange a tasting bar, serving creative cocktails or unique whiskeys, for the 21-and-up set, or hot cocoa and a coffee bar with toppings and treats. A photo booth filled with playful props will entertain guests of all generations. An interactive dessert station, like s'mores or ice cream sundaes, is sure to tempt. A table of activities for kids, from a scavenger hunt to no-mess crafts, will keep them occupied while their parents hit the dance floor.

YOUR GRAND EXIT

The wedding may be over, but your marriage is just beginning. As you make your departure from the reception, surround yourselves with the love of your family and friends, taking in those final moments before the day comes to an end. Select a meaningful last song, inviting your guests to join you on the dance floor one last time before the lights come on. Or, for a dramatic exit with sparklers, glow sticks, or ribbon wands, have guests head outside to wait for your grand exit while you and your new spouse share a last dance in private, just the two of you soaking up all of the memories before you head to your getaway car. While it is always bittersweet to have such a wonderful celebration come to an end, planning a few final moments that will stick in your mind for years to come is the perfect way to bring the evening to a close.

"There is magic in the moment when two people profess their love for one another, and that magic should look as incredible as it feels."

PART
TWO

ROMANTIC

Floral and feminine with a bit of whimsy

———————

For the romantic at heart, nothing compares to the beauty and sentiment evoked by a wedding. Taking a cue from the rose gold and morganite ring, a romantic wedding style is all about love. Dreamy florals, flowing gowns, and a color palette in shades of pink make the romantic style timeless and enchanting.

A DREAM COME TRUE

Your love story is the stuff of fairy tales, and your wedding day should be, too. These stories of true love are full of romance, the perfect inspiration for a wedding celebration. Whether you spent your childhood dreaming of fairies and Prince Charming or it was love at first sight when you found your own prince, your wedding day should be an opportunity to write a new chapter in an age-old story.

Bring the story to life with delicate details. Select a wedding gown in sweet lace and soft tulle, pick a palette in pretty pastels paired with eucalyptus and dusty miller, and choose a venue that seems worn by time, alluding to the romances of the past that have found their start in the same spot.

SOFT VOLUME Give your bouquet a dose of romance with an organic, cascading style in a soft palette. Pale pink roses and peonies surround fluffy Queen Anne's lace, with long-stemmed pink tulips creating volume and movement.

ROMANCE OF YORE For a celebration straight out of a fairy tale, combine time-worn stonework with romantic lace, a eucalyptus bouquet tied with trailing ribbons, and a floral crown fit for a fairy queen atop loose curls. **PRINCELY ENSEMBLE** Top a traditional tux with a boutonniere straight out of a storybook. Stephanotis, eucalyptus, and (quite fittingly) blushing bride protea come together for a bouquet that's textural, unique, and tells a story. **BALLGOWN FOR A PRINCESS** This lush and layered ballgown oozes romance. Tiers of tulle and lace give the gown fullness beneath a fitted lace bodice, with a small train perfect for an elegant entrance. An organic bouquet in shades of cream and peach complete the fairy tale ensemble.

SWEET NOTHINGS

Sometimes the simplest accessories are all it takes. Whether you're looking for a relaxed vibe, have a gown that makes a statement, or aren't really the "accessories" type, keeping things small and delicate will help you achieve a look you love.

Start with the classics, like a neutral shoe or a delicate pendant necklace—pieces you might wear on a day-to-day basis so you still feel like yourself. For a look that is romantic and just a bit trendy, a crown, whether beaded or made of fresh flowers, can create visual interest without the drama of a detailed veil. Try everything on in advance of your wedding so you can decide what works and what feels like too much, tweaking the combination until you're completely in love.

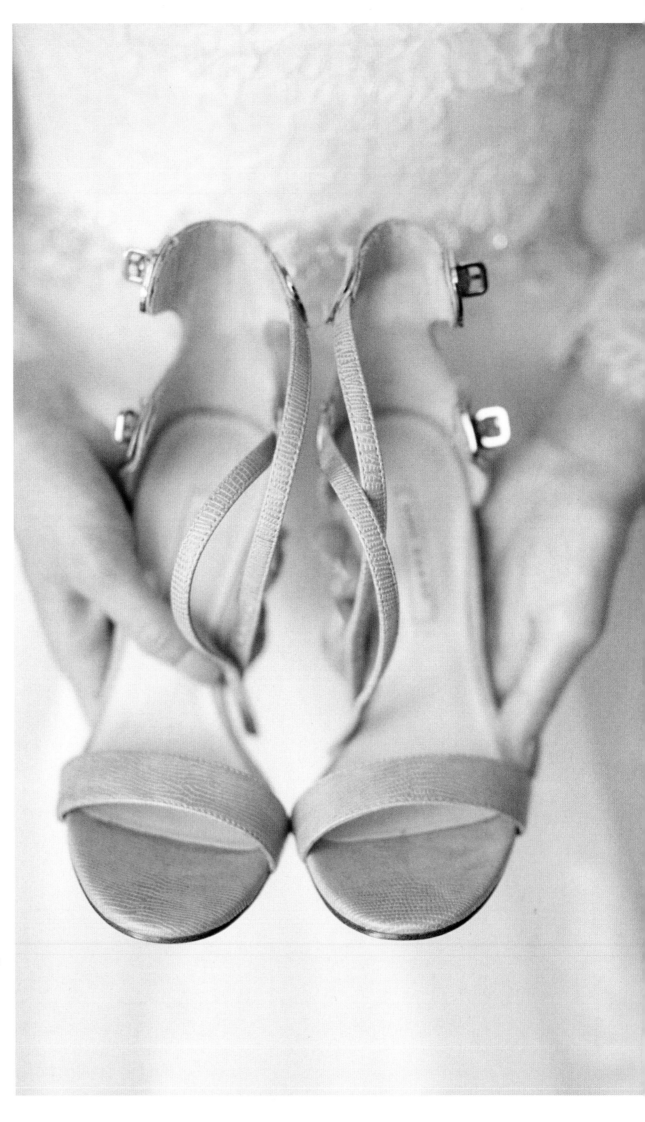

DELICATE SANDALS Let your dress shine by embracing classic neutrals in your accessories. A sandal or pump that matches your skin tone will elongate legs—or completely disappear beneath your gown.

SWEET ROYALTY Have a princess moment by topping your wedding hairstyle with a crown. This combination of crystals, leaves, and flowers is feminine and romantic, with just a touch of shine. DON SOME BLOOMS A sweet and simple flower crown has a romantic, just-picked feel. Stick with just a few blooms and some greenery to add a touch of color without overwhelming your style.

"I always try to find harmony in the details. Look for sparkle, dignity, and balance in every piece you pair."

DAINTY JEWELRY When working with large, voluminous flowers, keep your accessories minimal. A delicate bracelet won't compete with these peonies' major statement.

FEEL THE LOVE

Love is in the air! While you're working to personalize your wedding celebration, think about ways you can also infuse a few sentimental touches that will bring you right back to that moment, no matter how many years have passed.

Seek out meaningful gifts to share with your partner and your loved ones, selecting something that reflects both the occasion and their interests so they'll truly treasure it. Personalized accessories, such as monogrammed cufflinks or birthstone jewelry, are thoughtful go-to options. And don't forget to pick out a little something for yourself! You will remember your wedding day with a smile every time you see it.

LIGHT OF LOVE You may choose to honor cherished loved ones by lighting a candle during the ceremony. An heirloom candlestick can make this tradition especially meaningful. **PERSONALIZED DETAILS** Commemorate your big day with a sweet engraved charm. Clip it to your bouquet during the ceremony, then transfer it to a charm bracelet or keychain to keep with you always. **STYLED VOWS** Turn your vows into a keepsake by asking a calligrapher to transcribe them in flowing script. Tuck the vows into envelopes, seal with wax, and open them on a milestone anniversary. **SENTIMENTAL SCENT** Scent is one of our strongest memories, so take your time choosing the perfect perfume for your wedding day. Wear the fragrance your partner always associates with you, or pick something new so you'll go straight back to your wedding day every time you spray it on.

A FLORAL FRAME

Nothing says "romance" quite like an abundance of gorgeous flowers. Create an enchanted garden at your ceremony with a lush and fragrant floral arch, surrounding you and your partner in beauty as you exchange vows. Pair full and fresh flowers like soft peonies, fluffy hydrangeas, or sculptural dahlias with trailing greenery for an altar that appears to have grown naturally in its place. Look for altars in unique shapes or modern materials to give your romance a contemporary spin, or stick to the classics with a spectacular floral display that will make guests swoon.

WREATHED IN ROSES
Cascading flowers and draped greenery soften any structure, whether it's warm wood or more modern metal. A worn stone wall, lush plants, and sun shining at just the right angle will all come together for a gorgeous first kiss.

CREATE A CLUSTER Concentrate the majority of the flowers in one corner of your arch for an asymmetric display that oozes organic romance. Mix full blooms like hydrangeas and dahlias with smaller spray roses or ranunculus for eye-catching changes in scale.

"Your wedding day is your chance to star in your own love story, so fill it with romance to the nth degree!"

CIRCULAR SHAPE Surround yourselves with a circular altar, festooned with lush flowers and verdant greenery. This wider shape makes sure there's room for everyone at the top of the aisle and gives you extra real estate to create an even bigger floral statement.

GET OUTSIDE

Summer is the most popular season for weddings, and with good reason. When the weather cooperates, an outdoor wedding in the sunshine is breathtaking! When you're scouting outdoor locations, consider asking your photographer to tag along to help you pick the best angle and time of day for those perfectly warm photos—and make sure the sun won't be shining right into your guests' eyes during the ceremony. Look for locations with a bit of drama, whether it's surrounding flora or gorgeous architecture, or create your own beautiful atmosphere.

WOODED RETREAT Seeking the perfect spot for your ceremony? Look for a secluded location that lends an air of fantasy. Mix in a dreamy walkway, floral arbor, and tower of beautiful trees, and you have got the recipe for some serious newlywed romance.

STATELY GARDENS It's all in the details. This simple fountain pairs manicured gardens, a Pegasus sculpture, and the façade of a historic home, a setting that's straight out of a fairy tale. If your venue doesn't offer so much drama, look to a nearby park or public space for a short and sunny walk before the reception.

FAIRY TALE STATEMENTS
Tying the knot in a romantic
garden? Go all in with a striking
tone-on-tone palette and
enchanted accents. A butterfly
wing altar, shades of pink
blooms in lucite boxes, and
modern velvet seating are an
unexpectedly romantic take on
this classic setting. **LOVE'S
MEMORIAL** What's more
romantic than a pond with a
circular, colonnaded structure
situated right in the middle.
Look for these outdoor landmarks
that feel straight out of a dream.
TWINKLING LIGHTS Whether
you're in the heart of a city or
the outskirts of the countryside,
outdoor patios are the perfect
oasis for a reception. Guests
have the comfort of solid
footing with the fresh air that
makes feelings of love and joy
swell through atmosphere. An
abundance of hanging lights
draped over the tables adds
to the romance.

LOVE LETTERS

Receiving a hand-addressed envelope in the mail is inherently romantic, but wait until your guests see what is inside the envelope. Use carefully selected fonts and textured accents to transform a traditional suite into a love-filled invitation they won't want to turn down.

If your budget allows, work with a calligrapher to create hand lettering specifically for your suite, using the same style to address each envelope and escort card. For a more budget-friendly option, browse the web and find a font that makes your heart skip a beat.

When it comes to accents, less is more: a hint of color, a touch of metallic, or a perfectly placed floral accent will amp up the refined romance vibe.

TIME-WORN LOVE It's hard to resist the romance of handmade details, whether it's the painted edge of deckled paper or swirling hand-written calligraphy. The combination of gray, gold, and cream gives this suite an Old World feel.

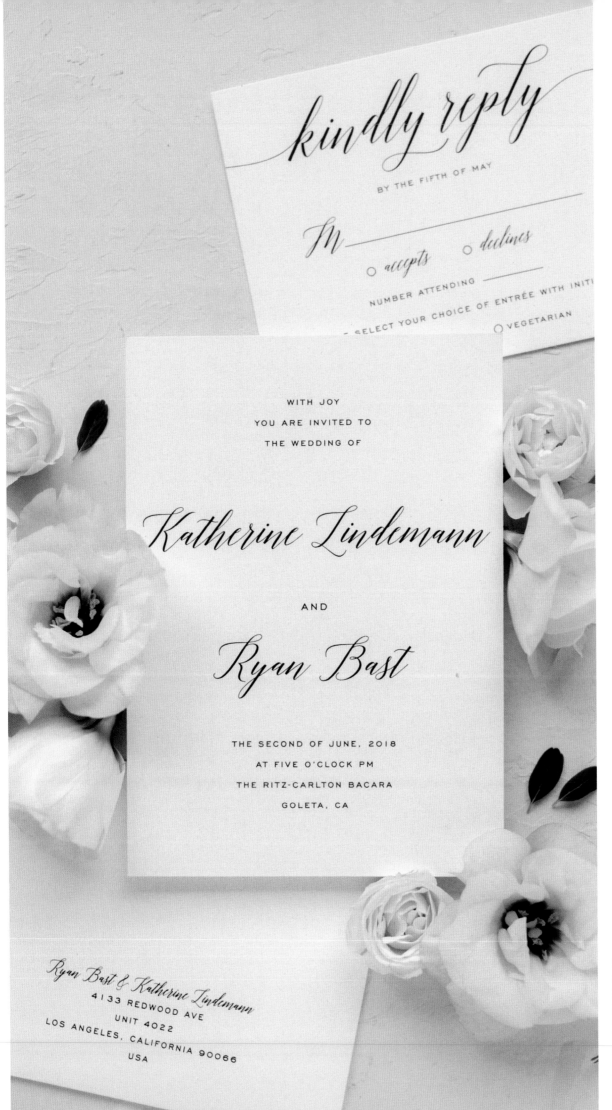

kindly reply

BY THE FIFTH OF MAY

M_____

○ accepts   ○ declines

NUMBER ATTENDING _____

SELECT YOUR CHOICE OF ENTRÉE WITH INITI

○ VEGETARIAN

WITH JOY
YOU ARE INVITED TO
THE WEDDING OF

Katherine Lindemann

AND

Ryan Bast

THE SECOND OF JUNE, 2018
AT FIVE O'CLOCK PM
THE RITZ-CARLTON BACARA
GOLETA, CA

Ryan Bast & Katherine Lindemann
4133 REDWOOD AVE
UNIT 4022
LOS ANGELES, CALIFORNIA 90066
USA

SWEET AND SIMPLE To create a feeling of contemporary romance on your invitation suite, pair your favorite style of modern calligraphy with a sleek sans serif font. The beauty is in the minimalist details.

BOUQUET LOVE STORY

Bouquets are more than just a few flowers to hold—they're an accessory that will further elevate your wedding day look. If romance is what you have in mind, seek out a bouquet that's soft in shape, full of lush and open blooms, and finished with the perfect trailing accents.

Roses, garden roses, and peonies are the iconic romantic bouquet trifecta, effortlessly enhanced with a few lisianthus, jasmine vine, and the perfect muted greenery. An organic shape allows vines to trail easily, creating a "just picked" feeling. Soften the final product with dramatic lengths of hand-dyed silk ribbon in a neutral tone. Now cue that warm mid-ceremony breeze!

"Trends may come and go, but love and romance are timeless."

SOFTLY FEMININE Layer details for an incredibly romantic statement. Pair a lace dress, off-the-shoulder neckline, soft curls, and a lush bouquet of garden roses and eucalyptus to write the next chapter of your love story.

RIPPLING RIBBONS There is nothing more perfect than bouquets overflowing with peonies. Tie the stems in dyed silk ribbon to catch the breeze, and set the bridal bouquet apart with hints of pink and a grander scale.

CASCADING BOUQUET
A pastel-toned combination of garden roses and peonies is sweet on its own, but the addition of trailing vines is what gives a bouquet that romantic feeling. Jasmine vine, smilax, and seeded eucalyptus add volume and movement.

ENCHANTING EUCALYPTUS
Love eucalyptus? Use a few different types to really get your fix. Here, silver dollar, seeded, and blue varietals add their own unique shapes to a soft and sweet bouquet.

CHARMING TABLE SETTINGS

Creating a romantic table is all about adding softness everywhere you can. Overblown blooms, pale pastels, and light and airy finishes are swoon-worthy ingredients!

Keep your color palette simple with just a few shades of white and pink. Add dusty rose or pale blue for a touch of contrast, mixing in classic silver for a fresh feel or gold for Old World warmth. Use organic greenery to brighten up each arrangement, turning to soft filler like sweet peas and astilbe for extra texture.

And don't forget the finishing touches! Handwritten place cards on paper scrolls, color-coordinated candles and glassware, and fresh flowers set on each napkin show that no detail has gone unaccounted for.

PASTELS AND NEUTRALS A pastel palette immediately adds romance to a table. Choose a subtle shade of pink, then use it for the napkins, the flowers, and even the matching taper candles. Set against a neutral tablecloth and white dishware, it's a soft but striking style.

TEXTURED GLASS Play with texture to create a table that's light and airy. Clear glassware in a variety of patterns will subtly enhance the texture of the ceramic centerpieces. An overflowing display of greenery, studded with roses, gives the table a "straight from the garden" feeling.

CANDLELIT TABLES Nothing says "romance" like candlelight, so scatter a mix of votives and taper candles down the table to bathe your guests in the flattering glow. Gold accents will pick up and enhance the warmth even further.

TABLESCAPE BOUQUETS Repurpose bouquets as centerpieces, and build your table design around this arrangement. Gold flatware and pastel pink linens and plates complement the blush and peach florals.

SWEET CONFECTIONS

Let them eat cake! These towering confections of pillowy pastry and sweet icing are the perfect ending to a celebratory meal, and all it takes is a few fresh and feminine touches to transform a wedding cake into a centerpiece that makes your heart skip a beat.

Fresh flowers and soft texture add the perfect hint of romance to a cake, bringing a note of freshness and delicate detail to the design. From simple ruffles to intricate piping, a little buttercream can go a long way. Or focus on the blooms, with cascades of roses (or whatever blossom your heart desires) enhancing the sweet canvas. Choose a flavor, or a few, that is equally lovely, and you'll be serving up dessert fit for a queen.

SATIN AND SOFT METALLICS
Dress up a simple wedding cake with fresh flowers and a little bit of shine. Satin ribbons around the top two tiers subtly pop against white fondant, while the gold-painted trim around the bottom perfectly matches each gilded berry.

FLOWING FLORALS AND GREENERY Create a soft, romantic cascade by adding strands of silver dollar eucalyptus to an arrangement of fresh blooms. Tuck them onto a subtly textured white cake for delicate, feminine contrast. **SWIRLING DETAIL** Pair piping with fresh flowers for a double dose of texture. These swirling rosettes and buttercream stars are a perfect match for the pale pink of the spray rose topper.

BRIMMING WITH ROSES
If you can't decide between a cake covered in hand-piped icing and a cascade of fresh roses, have both! Choose a subtle color for the buttercream so it nearly blends into the cake, letting the three-dimensional texture make the real statement.

LAVISH

Glam luxury and abundance

———————

A lavish ring makes a statement with size and sparkle,
and so does a lavish wedding. Sensational and steeped
in glamour, a lavish wedding is fit for a princess.
Cascading flowers, extravagant gowns, and plenty
of shimmering gold make this style absolutely
gorgeous and unforgettable.

A LUXE GOWN

All eyes will be on you as you walk down the aisle, so give your guests something to look at. An incredible bridal gown with all of the trimmings is a once-in-a-lifetime outfit you'll always remember.

Lavish wedding gowns range from sleek and sultry to voluminous, but they all share a few common traits. Carefully selected details will set the dress apart, from intricate beading or a wash of sparkles to heirloom lace and hand appliques. Finish your look with expert tailoring so your dress fits like a glove, and keep the accessories subtle so your dress—and the smile on your face—truly shines.

GLAMOROUS BALLGOWN
Nothing says "lavish wedding" quite like a spectacular ball gown. Look for a full skirt, a soft train, and luxe details like hand embroidery, three-dimensional appliques, or delicate lace (all of which give this barely blush gown by Be My White an ornate finish).

ACCESSORIES THAT SHINE

A few carefully chosen accessories will go a long way in helping you create an opulent, lavish wedding day look. A statement necklace, dangling earrings, or the perfect pair of shoes truly will bring everything together.

When you're looking to add a dose of sparkle, choose a classic shape to balance the bling. Look for a feminine collar necklace to sit above your collarbones, or a plunging pendant or lariat design to flatter a deep-V neckline. If you're wearing a statement necklace, keep your earrings small, or skip the necklace altogether and opt for a dangling earring design to frame your face.

A touch of shimmer on bridal shoes will put pep in your step as you walk down the aisle, from glitter fabric to crystal appliques—a great way to bring a bit of "you" into your wedding look.

WALK WITH A STATEMENT Glitter-covered shoes are fit for Cinderella—or a bride! Make your walk down the aisle extra special by tucking a secret message on your soles using adhesive letters, or ask your bridesmaids or future spouse to leave love notes to carry you to the altar.

BIG GLAM A little extra sparkle is always a good thing. If your gown is simple and sleek, add a touch of your personality with shimmering accessories, like a can't-miss statement necklace.

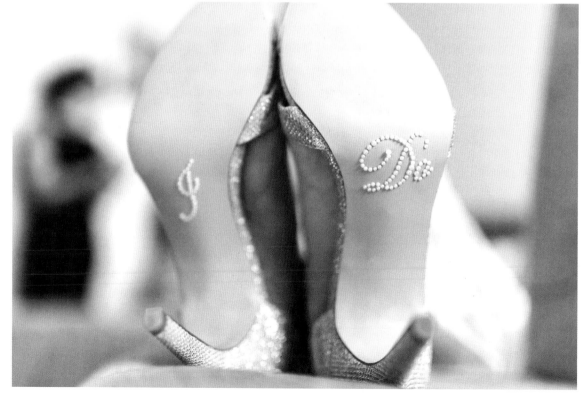

ELEGANT JEWELS When you are shopping for the perfect sparkling accessory in the faux jewelry department, look for refined styles that just might be real. A classic shape and solid setting will have your jewelry looking gorgeous, not gaudy.

SPARKLING PUMPS These d'Orsay pumps pair classic white satin with a little sparkle that makes them feel extra special. Subtle accents mean these shoes will work with almost any gown, and ankle straps keep them on your feet!

GIRLS IN GOLD

The best way to set the tone for a glamorous wedding celebration is by dressing your bridal party to the nines to match. Take traditional bridesmaids' dresses to the next level by trading tulle and chiffon for the unmistakable sparkle of sequins.

When choosing sequined wedding dresses, opt for a more classic silhouette so the fabric makes the biggest statement. Choose a metallic that matches your color palette, or—for extra drama— deck out your wedding in all white and have your bridesmaids wear a combination of rose gold, gold, and silver for a luxe and high-end finish. Keep the bouquets simple and modern so as not to compete with the gowns, resulting in a lavish and well-curated look.

OVER-THE-TOP GLAM
For a totally luxe take on a bridal party, dress your bridesmaids in head-to-toe gold sequins. Pair their dresses with cascading bouquets of white orchids for a modern look that shines.

A ROYAL AFFAIR

If you've always imagined being a princess one day, your wedding day is your moment. Put on your dream ball gown, top your curls with a tiara, and get ready for your grand entrance as you say "I do" to your Prince Charming.

Creating a royally inspired wedding day is all about tasteful choices. Pick a classic palette, choose a dress with a statement train and refined details, exchange vows in a spectacular venue, practice a waltz for your first dance, and select a luxury getaway car fit for a queen. Turn to recent royal weddings for your inspiration—those dukes and duchesses won't steer you wrong!

ROLL OUT THE RED CARPET
If you dream of marrying like a royal, choose a gown to match. A full skirt, ornate embroidery, and a statement-making, monarch-length train (over a yard long, though Kate Middleton's was nine feet and Princess Diana's was 25!) will ensure you make an entrance fit for a queen.

TIMELESS TUX There's nothing more luxe than a classic tuxedo with a satin lapel. Opt for a peak lapel and a matching bowtie for a traditional look, or choose a jacket with a shawl collar for a more modern take on this timeless attire.

"The royals have always been arbiters of style, so why not let their trips down the aisle inspire your own?"

GRAND EXIT Get to the church in style. A vintage car (plus a driver in a top hat!) is absolutely fit for royalty—just be sure to select a back seat that's spacious enough for a full ball gown and dramatic train.

A DOSE OF DRAMA

Couples hosting lavish weddings know that it's all about the drama. From choosing a venue to designing your cake, pick specific elements and moments where you can kick things up a notch in a way your guests will really notice.

Select the most statement-making of details to upgrade so your design feels indulgent, not over the top. This will also help stretch your budget, as you'll make an impact in the ways you love most without splurging on items that don't top your list of priorities. Just be sure other elements are well curated and thoughtfully selected so they feel intentional and cohesive, even if they're more subtle.

STRIKING GOWN Pair a grand venue with an equally grand gown. Lace, sparkles, and a beautiful shade of blush combine for an elegant gown that's finished with a dramatic train, ready for your walk down the aisle.
A SPECTACULAR PARTY All eyes on the dance floor! A massive chandelier fills this ballroom with sparkle and is the perfect shimmering frame for this couple's joy-inducing Hora and a dramatic chair lift.

DOUBLE DESSERT Why have just a cake when you can serve two desserts in one? This dramatic display features frosting-covered wedding cake topped with towers of sweet cream puffs. **AN IMPRESSIVE CAKE DISPLAY** Give a simple wedding cake a lavish treatment. Set the cake on a table draped in sequined linens, then cover the side of the cake with a gorgeous and fragrant cascade of roses.

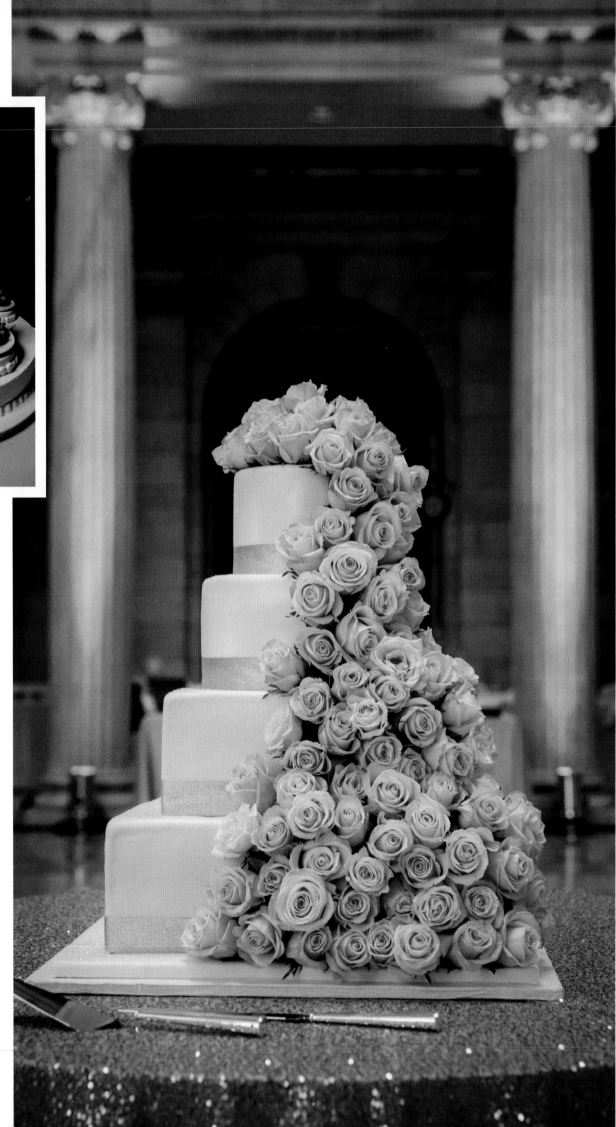

LOCATION, LOCATION, LOCATION

If you are looking to make a major statement at your wedding, start with a jaw-dropping venue that will have guests ooh-ing and aah-ing the moment they arrive. Opulent locations, such as historic mansions or far-off French chateaus, set a tone that truly can't be replicated. Seek out a venue that pairs a spectacular interior with gorgeous grounds or a unique natural environment to give your celebration a sense of place and grandeur.

Inside the reception, continue that feeling of drama with luxe finishes and layered details. Consider the décor from ceiling to floor— including the style of lighting, the texture of the linens, and even the flooring under your feet—so each element comes together to create an unforgettable wow-factor.

BOLD DRAPING Nothing transforms a tent quite like incredible draping, softening every corner of the space. With a carpeted floor and crystal chandeliers, your guests won't know if they are inside a grand ballroom or beneath a tent on a sprawling lawn.

The Biltmore Estate has views for days! A gorgeous chateau is itself photo worthy, but when paired with manicured lawns, pebbled drives, and mountains in the distance, it is a luxe and lavish setting fit for royalty.

"As you search for your dream venue, look for the elements that are unique, that make a place truly stand out, then use those details to make your wedding truly yours."

CELEBRATE IN SPLENDOR

Celebrate your marriage with a reception on a grand scale, with opulent finishes, from luxe fabrics to incredible flowers, as far as the eye can see. You'll only do this once, so why not go big?

Pair an ornate venue with a design scheme that fits perfectly, from the colors you choose to the style of the centerpieces. In a space that's more of a blank canvas, let your imagination run wild as you fill it with your wedding fantasy. A pared-down palette helps even the most lavish of designs feel refined and well curated, giving those statement elements a well-deserved place in the spotlight.

BAROQUE BALLROOM With a room as rich and opulent as this one, keep the tablescapes and centerpieces minimal. Muted anthurium and sculptural orchids perfectly match the neutral linens and colored taper candles, while pops of pink scabiosas add a modern feel to a classic space.

125

"I adore an opulent celebration. Whether you use your grandmother's fine china or rent something spectacular, now is the moment to really push your sensibility and take it to the next level."

FLOWERS EVERYWHERE Use flowers in unexpected ways, like covering the table with a thick carpet of hydrangeas instead of a fabric runner. The heady fragrance and soft appearance will make a major statement at dinner. **SOARING ARTWORK** For a lush and lavish design, start with an opulent ballroom. Elevated arrangements point to the beautiful folds of the drapes and the colorful and ornate ceiling. Keep the tables and chairs simple so the eye is drawn upward—and stays there.

GILD THE LILY

Nothing dresses up a wedding quite like the addition of gold accents. From the paper goods and place settings to your cake and even your dress, they give every detail an extra bit of shine, creating an opulent and totally lavish effect.

As you're choosing gilded details, be consistent with the shade of gold you use as the metal can range from warm and yellow to cool and almost silvery. Pick a gold that works best with the other colors you've selected for a cohesive palette. Play with fabrics, textures, and finishes to add depth and visual interest, and don't be afraid to add sequins or crystal for a little sparkle!

GOLDEN CAKE A dramatic, towering design with golden fondant takes this wedding cake to the next level. Ornate gold details and golden cord add extra texture against a smooth background.

SEQUINED DÉCOR A little sparkle can go a long way, so pair shimmering gold with classic white to give the gilded items even more punch. Pair sequins with textured linens for visual interest, and don't forget to match the chairs and cushions to the place settings. **MILK AND HONEY** Honey has long been a symbol of sweetness and love in a new marriage. Bring this tradition into your own celebration by placing a petite pot at each guest's seat with a glass of milk, a wish for your marriage and for your newly combined families. **GILDED MENAGERIE** Who says lavish accents can't be fun? When coated in gold paint, animal figurines become a posh and playful way to display guests' escort cards—as well as a cute keepsake for the end of the night. **FOILED PAPER GOODS** Pair gold foil-stamping with embossed text for a textured invitation suite that shines. Whether it's a modern monogram, simple framing, or a luxe Old World-inspired border, a metallic touch will hint at the lavish celebration to come.

OUTDOOR OPULENCE

Intricate texture and exquisite accents make a statement all their own, but when these ornate details are brought outdoors, it takes their impact to another level. Luxe furniture, fine fabrics, and lush and colorful floral arrangements—all arranged in a natural garden setting— will be the "wow" factor your guests won't stop talking about.

More is more in this instance, so don't be afraid to layer that opulence everywhere you look. Seek out antique furniture with striking hand-carved finishes, layer rich patterns in coordinating color palettes, and encourage all of your vendors (from the florist to the cake baker) to err on the side of extra. After all, you'll only be celebrating your wedding day once, so go big!

BAROQUE DETAILS Brocade fabrics are striking on their own, and become even more so when you layer similar patterns in contrasting colors. And nothing says turn-of-the-century opulence quite like gilded bird cages—though the live leopard is optional!

"Use your wedding as an opportunity to go the extra mile. Fancy things up a little bit to make them feel even more special!"

FANCY FRAMES Bring texture and detail into unexpected spaces, such as your escort card display. Collect intricate frames, then display them side-by-side to help guests find their seat as they're immersed in your lavish vision. **ORNATE CAKE** Your cake is the centerpiece of the reception, so make it a show-stopper! Use vibrant colors, lots of fresh flowers, and gilded accents for a dessert that stands out. **EXOTIC ANIMALS** Make your wedding day even more unforgettable with a few surprise guests. Work with a local zoo or conservation society to bring exotic animals to cocktail hour where guests can interact with these incredible creatures—and even learn a little something before dinner.

MODERN

Minimal, clean, and bright

With clean lines, crisp whites, and unconventional details, a modern wedding is striking and unique. Like the subtle addition of black diamonds to an engagement ring, modern weddings put a twist on the traditional. Geometric details, metallic finishes, and exotic flowers come together for a look that is singular in its simplicity.

STREAMLINED STYLE

Modern brides, rejoice! Ready-to-wear fashion is making its way into the bridal scene, providing sleek and on-trend options for both you and your bridesmaids.

As you're dressing yourself, look for a wedding gown with a streamlined silhouette and architectural accents to create a unique shape, then bring in your personality with a pair of statement shoes you adore—and that you will absolutely wear again. Keep accessories simple and your hair and makeup subtle and natural to showcase the best version of you.

For your bridesmaids, think outside the box and consider fashion-forward silhouettes and prints that your best friends will love wearing down the aisle.

UPDATED HEMLINE It's amazing how a short skirt can make a bride look instantly chic and modern. A big bow of gathered chiffon is a sweet style statement. Pair this off-the-shoulder neckline with pulled-back hair so everyone can see the asymmetrical details.
SLEEK SILHOUETTES Dress up a simple silhouette with sculptural draping to give a fuss-free wedding dress visual appeal. A wrapped bodice and belted waist will accentuate your figure, while a thigh-high slit is perfect for showing a little leg.

COLORFUL CONTRAST There is nothing more fun than a playful pair of shoes peeking out from beneath a wedding dress. These ruffled flamingo-inspired sandals by Sophia Webster pair modern lines with a punch of color. **DITCH THE DRESSES** For a modern take on bridal party attire, outfit your bridesmaids in convertible jumpsuits instead of dresses. The flowing pants keep things feeling formal, while the comfortable silhouette is made for dancing.

MOD MEN

Suits don't offer quite as many opportunities to put a modern spin on groom's attire, but that's where accessories come into play. A slight update to a classic piece can change your style from head to toe.

Ties are the perfect place to start, as even choosing between a straight tie and a bowtie can completely alter your look. Add in a unique color or print, and you will be ready to tie the knot in style. Socks are often an afterthought, but if you're usually more conservative, this mostly hidden accessory can be a fun way to play with color or a print without going overboard.

And don't forget the boutonniere! Update the classic floral pin with unique add-ins, or skip the flowers altogether in favor of a boutonniere made of greenery, organic materials like feathers, or a nonfloral pin made from fabric, leather, or even wood and metal.

NONTRADITIONAL BOUTONNIERES For a contemporary take on the boutonniere, combine traditional roses and berries with unique leaves and nonfloral accents. A feather can add color and softness, while a leaf with a dramatic cut-out becomes an eye-catching frame for a classic bloom.

PATTERNED POPS Move over, black tie! Give a suit a punch of personality with a creative tie alternative. Choose a color or pattern that coordinates with your wedding's design—think the floral palette or the bridesmaids' dresses—for a cohesive addition that really pops.

STATEMENT TIES Dress up a dark suit with a tie flaunting a bold floral pattern. Floral patterns have invaded the wedding space, from tablecloths to bridesmaids' dresses and even to wedding gowns, and a strong combination of colors makes it right at home on a sleek, skinny tie.

PLAYFUL SOCKS If statement patterns aren't your style, turn to creative socks instead. You'll still look classic, but lift a pant leg and you can flaunt the perfect amount of (subdued) flare. Pick a pattern for all of the groomsmen to wear, or choose a playful sock to match each gentleman's personality.

CENTER STAGE

Truly set the scene with a dramatic statement wall. This spectacular display is perfect for a ceremony backdrop, behind the band, or for the ultimate wedding selfies with your guests.

A statement wall can take all different shapes, whether it's an organic display of flowers and greenery, a unique combination of fabrics and paper, a cascade of lights, or a perfectly placed garland against reclaimed wood or another textured material. For a fun finish, add a neon sign with your new last name or a quote from your favorite movie in swirling calligraphy. Use your statement wall to enhance your palette, create a stunning focal point, and frame the most memorable moments of your wedding day.

STATEMENT-MAKING SHAPES
Exchange vows in front of a statement living wall covered in bold lines and vibrant leaves. Each section, filled with a single type of greenery, brings texture and color to this unique and photo-ready backdrop.

A MODERN FRAME Pair rustic materials with a modern shape for a ceremony that's all your own. A wooden hexagon, accented with blooms, bridges the gap beautifully. **FLORAL WALL** A display of tightly packed coral, blush, and peach flowers climbing up a solid wall of greenery is both colorful and contemporary. Flanked by sleek mirrored platforms topped with a cluster of flowers and candles, the modern and romantic styles merge beautifully.

STRUCTURED GREENS

Colorful flowers aren't the only option for your wedding's décor and accessories. Swap out piles of petals for sculptural accents in totally vibrant green. While some flowers, like hydrangeas and amaryllis, do come in a naturally green hue, it's more structured plants like orchids and succulents that truly shine. Their unique shapes give any arrangement a crisp and modern feel that is hard to achieve with other options. Layer multiple shades of green, including a variety of leaves and vines, to create depth and texture. Use succulents as a focal point, taking the place of a flower, or mix them in amongst a variety of blooms for a floral-like look. These hardy plants are fantastic as boutonnieres, as they survive well without water, and also make fantastic favors for guests to take home.

THE WHOLE BRANCH A branch of orchids is a unique alternative to a classic bouquet shape. Vibrant green and purple cymbidium orchids pop against deep green leaves. Add trailing vines for an organic effect, then carry the branch of blooms in your fingertips or tucked into one elbow. **DRAMATIC SHAPES** While calla lilies, hydrangeas, and roses are all right at home in a bouquet, the addition of a dramatic air plant takes this arrangement to the next level. The unique and dimensional shape wraps around the other blooms to give a more traditional bouquet a modern twist.

BABY SUCCULENT When setting a modern table, don't forget that finishing touch. A simple napkin fold over a brushed gold charger creates the perfect backdrop for a petite succulent—which your guests can take home and plant once your reception is over.

ALL GREEN BOUTONNIERE This "sempervivum" succulent has a distinct floral-like shape, making it ideal for a boutonniere. Look for a slightly smaller specimen so it fits nicely on the lapel, then add a bit of greenery to fill it out.

ACRYLIC ACCENTS

Fill your modern wedding with sheer delight. Acrylic pieces can make a dramatic statement—even though you can barely see them. Acrylic chairs give even the most classic of shapes a contemporary feel, letting the rest of the décor really shine. Consider acrylic seating at a ceremony with a dramatic backdrop (like a beach at sunset or a towering mountaintop), as the clear material will ensure everyone has a perfect view.

If you're looking to enhance your paper goods and signage, turn to acrylic panels with vinyl cut-outs or handwritten calligraphy. Layer each piece in front of a textured or colorful backdrop for easy reading.

GREEN GARLAND In a lush setting, use the existing nature to your advantage as a background for your acrylic seating chart. A garland draped across the top, whether solely greenery or studded with blooms, ensures guests won't miss it!

UNOBSTRUCTED VIEW

Seating charts are the perfect use for acrylic accents. Create a floating frame holding acrylic panels, decorated with brushed paint to make the calligraphy truly pop—perfect for a backdrop where the sea and the sky meet. **SPACIOUS SEATING** Keep your reception space feeling light and airy with tables surrounded by acrylic chairs, modeled after the Louis Ghost Chair created by Philippe Starck. The barely there material mimics the openness created by floor-to-ceiling windows, maintaining a spacious ambiance even if you're seating a crowd. **CLASSIC SHAPE, MODERN STYLE** Use acrylic chairs in an ornate, more traditional shape to bridge the gap between modern and classic. The luxe look instantly elevates a reception space without weighing it down with heavy-looking furniture.

GEOMETRIC LINES

Sharp lines and geometric shapes are instantly modern, creating a crisp and clutter-free setting for your celebration. Every detail has a place and a purpose—meaning you can focus on the party.

As you're assembling your modern vision, turn to geometric lines to help your design take shape—literally. Carry these shapes throughout your design, from the paper goods to the ceremony backdrop, to create cohesion. Seek similar shapes and lines in your décor, whether it's a modern lantern or a patterned linen, to bring the point home, then let the organic shapes of flowers and greenery add a touch of softness.

ENERGETIC GRAPHIC DESIGN
Layer textures, colors, and crisp lines for a modern invitation your guests will love. Mix sans serif fonts and sharp angles, repeating shapes throughout your suite to tie everything together.

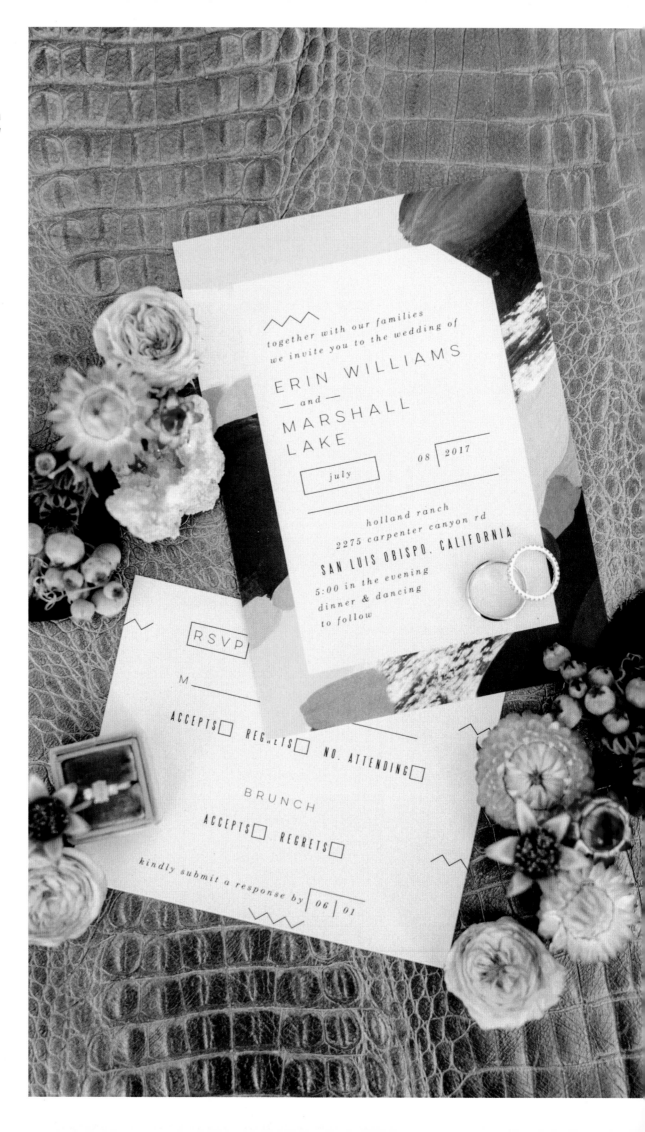

HEXAGONAL TABLE NUMBERS
Laser-cutting creates clean lines and a graphic look, no matter the material. Simple wood becomes a unique three-dimensional table number, with sharp edges and cut-outs for a modern finish. **STRUCTURAL ACCENTS** Look for accent pieces you can weave into your décor that will carry those crisp lines throughout your venue. Metal lanterns in a hexagonal shape will do just that, as well as cast a warm glow around floral arrangements or scattered along tabletops.

SERVICE WITH STYLE

New trends in service are turning wedding meals into entertainment all their own. Interactive stations and creative displays encourage guests to play with their food, and when that bite tastes as good as it looks, it's a memory in the making.

Buck the tradition of stuffy plated meals (and invite guests to get involved!) with family-style platters and DIY drinks or desserts. If they need a break from the dance floor, entice guests to gather around a donut bar or a mixologist shaking up specialty cocktails.

Tie these unique displays and creative service options into your décor by choosing designs that fit your theme, from a sleek dessert wall to a nostalgia-inducing camper-turned-bar.

LEAN IN Wow your guests with a gravity-defying dessert display, making finding a sweet treat an interactive adventure. A unique presentation gives even classic desserts, like bundt cakes and macarons, a modern edge.
OFF THE WALL Is there anything more beloved than a donut? Whether you're tying the knot at a morning wedding or are serving your favorite breakfast as a late-night snack, guests will flock to a wall covered in these spherical sweets.
MIMOSAS ANYONE? Have your table numbers do double duty, helping guests find their seats and fueling the party. Set each place with a glass of champagne, then serve up a sleek carafe of your favorite juice for an extra-festive toast.
COCKTAIL CARAVAN Have a little fun with your beverage service by slinging drinks out of the side of a totally adorable restored camper. You'll be able to set up wherever suits your celebration—just make sure it's picturesque for those selfies your guests are sure to be snapping!

ICING ON THE CAKE

Modern wedding cakes pair designs and details that truly set them apart. From unique shapes to playful colors and textures, it's a far cry from wedding cakes of the past.

When designing a modern wedding cake, begin first with a sleek shape. Clean lines and sharp edges will create the perfect canvas for your sweet vision. From there, get creative with colors, techniques, and finishes to set your cake apart. Top it off with sculptural blooms (whether fresh or actually sculpted from gum paste), and don't forget to put an equally unique flavor inside! Look for a baker with a portfolio that stands out from the crowd, with exciting and fresh designs alongside classic shapes and styles.

CONTRASTING CAKE This isn't your grandmother's wedding cake. With a matte black finish, a gilded deckled edge, and vibrant red sugar ranunculus (not to mention a sleek square shape), this sweet treat is decidedly modern. **CRISP ROUNDS** Put a contemporary spin on a more classic design with a few updated details. Keep the finish clean and smooth, give each tier an extra-sharp corner, and add metallic starbursts for a hint of shine.

HAND PAINTED TIERS An artist's interpretation of a wedding cake, hand-brushed color gives these tiers eye-catching texture. Subtle embellishment from scattered sugar pearls puts all the focus on this cake's unique finish and calming color. **OMBRÉ IS HERE TO STAY** Softly airbrushed pink pigment fades to white on this petite, single-tiered wedding cake. A crown of macarons in perfectly matching hues, plus a ruffled handmade sugar peony, would make this cake stand out on a dessert display.

GO TROPICAL

If you are heading to the beach for a destination wedding in the sun, infuse your oceanfront celebration with a modern vibe by focusing on statement-making greenery instead of intricate blooms. Palm fronds, monstera leaves, and other locally foraged accents will give your celebration an unmistakable sense of place.

This vibrant accent says modern thanks to its eye-catching scale and high-contrast color. The leaves seem larger-than-life, whether you're carrying one as a bouquet or using it in place of a traditional charger on your reception tables. Against a white dress and soft white sand, they are an easy accent that will take your design to the next level.

MEGA MONSTERA Who needs tropical flowers when you can make a major statement with a single leaf? Skip the bouquet and carry a dramatic monstera leaf down the aisle—the deep green tone will totally pop against a white wedding dress.

"Look for a single detail that will create consistency throughout your design. It creates harmony and balance– but doesn't have to be boring!"

PAPER GOODS THAT POP Invitations give your guests a hint at the celebration to come, and this suite screams "tropical getaway." A single leaf makes a statement on the invitation, while peeks of greenery on the RSVP card and ceremony program keep the theme going. **SUMMER STYLE** Bridal flats can still be high fashion, and these strappy Valentinos are a modern beach bride's dream shoe. Pair them with fresh flowers and local greenery for a detail shot that will take you right back to the beach.

IN YOUR FAVOR

Show your guests how much you appreciate their presence with a sweet favor that will remind them of your wedding day. To put a modern spin on the tradition, skip monogrammed tchotchkes in favor of thoughtful gifts they'll appreciate—and really use.

Edible favors are a fantastic first choice, whether it's a late-night snack for the ride home or something sweet to enjoy in the morning. For something that might last a little longer, consider plants and seeds—they're an eco-friendly options, and your guests will remember your celebration every time they see what their green thumbs have created. Still can't decide? Instead of buying something, use that money to make a donation to a charity you care about. Print a sign letting guests know you've made a donation in their honor, along with a note about how and why you chose the organization.

PLANT A SEED If you've got a green thumb, get guests in on the fun by inviting them to create their own seed mix to plant at home. Be sure to provide tips for sunlight and watering so your loved ones can have lots of garden success.

POTTED DECORATION No green thumb? No problem! Succulents and cacti are hardy and resistant—and happen to look fantastic on a desk or windowsill. Choose your favorite varieties, tuck them into miniature pots, and send them home with your guests with care instructions.

ELEGANT

Timeless beauty and grace

————————

Elegance never goes out of fashion. Like a classic diamond engagement ring, it is beautiful, enduring, and always in style. Gracious and refined, an elegant wedding features the timeless looks that speak to sophistication and tradition. A white gown in a classic silhouette, bouquets of white roses, and impeccable venues are the hallmarks of an elegant wedding.

A TIMELESS BRIDE

Find elegance in simplicity. When paired with a loving smile and a bit of unbridled excitement, a simple fabric, a few carefully selected details, and a crisp and clean finish are all it takes to make a striking statement as you walk down the aisle.

When shopping for an elegant wedding gown, choose just a few subtle accents to set your gown apart, whether it's a classic silhouette in a textured fabric or the addition of delicate lace or tulle to soften a sleek gown. Turn to timeless design and expert tailoring to create an ethereal ensemble that will let you shine, knowing that less can truly be more.

STRUCTURED YET FLOWING
Feminine details add an elegant finish to a classic wedding dress. A structured overskirt with horsehair trim and a cascading veil, paired with a petite bouquet and a timeless chignon, take this simple strapless gown to new heights.

TRAILING TRAINS

Instantly add elegance to your wedding gown by choosing a dress with a flowing train. A chapel-length train gives a wedding dress presence while still being easy to maneuver and to bustle later in the evening, making this mid-length train ideal for an elegant wedding. Should you prefer, the bustle can be replaced with a wrist loop that will allow you to lift your skirt as you move around. If you prefer a longer train for a dramatic trip down the aisle, work with your seamstress to create a secure bustle so you can dance with ease! From short and sweet to long and dramatic, a train will help any bride make an entrance—and an exit.

FEMININE, CHAPEL-LENGTH TRAIN During the ceremony, your guests will see the back of your dress more than the front. A sweet chapel-length train and a lace overlay are pretty and feminine touches that give your guests something gorgeous to look at as you exchange vows.

LOVELY VEIL When choosing your veil to wear over a dress with a train, make sure your dress and veil are of different lengths. A shorter veil, such as a waltz or elbow, will float elegantly around your body, while a longer veil will cover your train and glide down the aisle behind you, making an elegant statement. **HOLD THE TRAIN** After your walk down the aisle, plan for a graceful way to prevent your train from dragging on the ground. A seamstress can add a strap so you can hook it to your wrist, or can install a traditional bustle—your train will begin to feel heavy at the end of your long and exciting day.

BEST DRESSED

Is there anything more handsome than a man in a perfectly tailored tuxedo? For an elegant wedding with a black tie dress code, a tux is the only way to go—but it doesn't have to be boring. Today's tuxedos feature modern fits and updated accents. Play with fabrics, collar shapes, and even colors to create a unique ensemble that will give James Bond a run for his money. The secret to a jaw-dropping tuxedo, though, is all in the tailoring. Turn to a professional who will make sure every point of the tuxedo fits perfectly. Whether it's fully custom or affordable and off the rack, if it's tailored well, no one will be able to tell the difference.

Finally, don't forget the accessories! Leave memories of prom tuxes in the past with a refined boutonniere, statement-making shoes, and an heirloom-worthy watch and cufflinks.

STACY & FILIP
SEPTEMBER 2, 2018

CLASSIC ELEGANCE They're classics for a reason. A black satin bow tie, a silver watch and cufflinks, and an elegant white ranunculus boutonniere are iconic finishing touches for a groom in a tuxedo. Just don't forget to put your vows in your perfectly tailored jacket pocket!

WELL GROOMED Set the tone for a formal evening with groomsmen all in tuxedos. The groom might stand out with the addition of a vest, a different collar shape, or a more stately boutonniere, but if he's in a tux, his groomsmen should be, too.

TIE YOUR OWN Pre-tied bow ties may be convenient, but a self-tied version carries unmistakable elegance. Just be sure to practice tying your bow tie before your wedding day (and find a handy video online if wedding day jitters wipe your memory).

SIGNATURE SHOES Who says dress shoes have to be black and shiny? Add a touch of personality by seeking out unique dress shoes that speak to your style, whether it's a combination of fabrics, the use of unique colors, an elegant monk strap, or a chic smoking slipper.

MEN IN NAVY

While black tie may be the first thought when selecting elegant menswear for your wedding, consider navy suits and tuxedos to create a feeling of relaxed elegance and give your celebration a more modern twist.

For a black tie event, don a navy tuxedo with a black lapel and bowtie. The contrast in colors gives the style a subtle pop, and is the perfect choice for a fashion-forward groom when paired with a shawl collar and matte black dress shoes. If "understated elegance" is your goal, ask the groom and groomsmen to don matching navy suits, which you can pair with brown accessories (and even a printed tie) for an easygoing, polished group.

FASHIONABLE TUX It may not seem like a big leap, but a navy tuxedo is definitely the fashion-forward choice when it comes to formalwear. Keep the accessories classic (think a black satin bow tie and a traditional boutonniere) if the groom is ready for the aisle, but not the runway.

IDENTICAL SUITS While asking groomsmen to wear their own navy suits may sound easy, it can result in a variety of shades that is at home at a more casual celebration. To keep things buttoned up, ask them to rent or purchase the same suit, ensuring flawless matching.

SUMMERY ENSEMBLE A lighter tie is perfect for a spring or summer wedding. Muted beige plays nicely with brown shoes, or you could select a patterned tie that picks up the color of the bridesmaids' dresses for something a little more playful.

POLISHED CAKES

Intricate icing and lush flowers have their place, but at an elegant wedding a simple and sophisticated cake will steal the show. Whether you're using rolled fondant or crisp buttercream, the addition of a subtle hint of texture and a few carefully placed blooms are all it takes to make this sweet treat a star.

The beauty of an all-white wedding cake is that the interior can still be as playful and creative (or as classic) as you'd like. Imagine guests' surprise when, at the end of your black tie celebration, they're served a delicious funfetti cake studded with a rainbow of sprinkles! Even the most elegant of cakes should flaunt a bit of personality.

REFINED GREENERY Dress up a silky smooth wedding cake by pairing fondant flowers with a cascade of fresh ivy. Gently drape the greenery so it appears to have grown over the cake, letting the hand-cut sugar blossoms shine.

ALL-WHITE TEXTURE A little texture goes a long way. Subtle striped buttercream and perfectly placed Swiss dots dress up this simple, all-white confection without any fuss.

WHITE FLORALS

Wedding floral design runs the gamut from crisp and manicured to flowing and organic, all with beautiful results. What's one foolproof way to give whatever style you choose an instantly elegant finish? Opt for a monochromatic, all-white color palette.

By working with flowers in a single color, every arrangement immediately appears polished. The design can be toned down with the use of just a single bloom, or given lush texture by pairing a wide variety of flowers, all in the same color. The nearly endless variety of blooms to choose from means you can select a combination that best fits your vision, knowing that classic white wedding flowers will stand the test of time.

TEXTURED BOUTONNIERE
A white boutonniere is totally classic. Swap out the traditional rose for a ruffled ranunculus, which adds subtle texture and a more modern finish. Use a knot of white ribbon to tie on a sprig of dark greenery, then place these on a sleek black lapel.

UNSTRUCTURED VARIETY Use lots of textured flowers to make an all-white bouquet an exciting option. Pair dahlias, peonies, roses, lisianthus, and white lilacs for a gorgeous combination of size and shapes. **CRISP QUADRANTS** For a crisp and elegant statement, this densely packed arrangement combines clusters of four different all-white blooms for maximum impact. **ELEGANT BOUQUET** For a slightly more structured bouquet, begin with a base of crisp calla lilies. Sweet peas add a bit of softness, while seeded eucalyptus creates a whimsical finish for your tasteful bouquet.

IN NEUTRAL TERRITORY

Paring down your palette to a variety of neutral tones is instantly elegant and sophisticated. Whether you go warm with dove gray, oatmeal, and ivory, or opt for a cooler palette with steely undertones, it is amazing how much depth you can achieve with just a few simple colors. Using a range of neutral colors, instead of a monochromatic white palette, creates an inviting and lived-in ambiance that will immediately make your guests feel at home.

Use linens, dishware, and paper goods to help bring this palette to life. Look for options that offer unique texture, whether it's the nubby feel of a handwoven napkin or dinner plates with a striking matte finish. For the centerpieces, keep flowers neutral as well, using whites and creams for a bit of organic warmth and lots of greenery for a single pop of vibrance.

GORGEOUS GRAYS Layer a variety of neutral shades in a matching texture—such as shades of oat and gray in washed linen—to add depth to your table while keeping the setting comfortable and relaxed. **LAYERED WHITES** For a lighter take, turn to shades of white and top with greenery-heavy centerpieces. And don't forget the chairs! Pick a coordinating gray tone in a high-texture finish for a totally chic setting.

NEUTRAL CONTRAST
Make a major statement with contrasting paper goods. Choose an off-white paper and dove gray ink for your invitations, then flip-flop the colors with dove gray envelopes and off-white calligraphy.

WEARABLE WHITE These aren't your mother's white satin shoes! High-end designers are offering their signature styles in shades of white and a variety of fabrics so you can walk down the aisle in serious style.

SOOTHING SPACE Warm neutrals are oh-so-soothing. Seek out a bridal suite with cozy tones of taupe, stone, and ivory so you can get glam and stay zen. The soft palette is the perfect backdrop for bridal party photos!

POLISHED ELEGANCE

It's all in the details. If you're hosting an elegant wedding in an outdoor setting, incorporate ornate accents that are a perfect fit for your venue. Let the location inspire you, choosing a palette and style that take the venue's existing attributes to the next level. Starting with a venue that makes a statement on its own will make dressing the space to the nines even easier.

Create a feeling of intimacy with candlelit centerpieces, whimsical lighting (hello, hanging lanterns!), and swaths of greenery. The key is in the details—even the smallest of accents should be carefully considered and upgraded to put the finishing touches on a feeling of polished elegance.

QUAINT SEATING A tunnel of overgrown greenery is adorned with white lanterns and chairs, creating a perfect space for guests to escape for quiet conversations.

MARBLED ACCENTS In the right material, even simple accents can make a statement. Elevate your table numbers by replacing standard paper or frames with hand calligraphy on white marble. **TOUCHES OF GLAM** A simple wedding cake gets a good dose of glamour when set on the right cake stand. A few perfectly placed crystals will catch the light as the flash goes off during the cake cutting. **CLASSIC CANDLES** Mercury glass candlesticks in a classic shape anchor floral centerpieces, bringing warmth and a touch of elegance to the table. **GORGEOUS GREENHOUSE** A conservatory setting comes with its own lush greenery. Add twinkling lights to soften the angular planes of the roof.

ESTATE OF GRACE

There's nothing like a stately venue to truly set the scene for your wedding celebration. Grand estates have inherent style, requiring little to transform them into an elegant setting for a reception. From sweeping staircases and crawling ivy to high ceilings and manicured gardens, most of the design work is done for you!

The appeal of an estate venue is the sense of place it creates. As you're touring, keep an eye open for the perfect ceremony backdrop, a stunning scene for portraits, and private corners where you and your partner can sneak away for a moment alone. Let the details of the venue inspire the rest of your décor, whether it's the choice of linens or the color of the flowers, to create a cohesive and immersive experience.

STUNNING SETTINGS Add a serious dose of romance to your wedding album with photos you can't get anywhere else. A balcony covered in ivy (with a wrought iron door to boot) is a can't-miss opportunity for a couple's portrait!

GRACIOUS GROUNDS Whether it's perfectly manicured or wild and overgrown, an estate garden is the ideal place for wandering with a glass of champagne during cocktail hour. Let the flowers inspire the blooms you choose for your bouquet and centerpieces. **GARDEN GATES** Pretty gates and gravel drives transport guests to another time and place. If you are seeking a ceremony spot on-property, consider using that long driveway as your aisle for a statement-making entrance. **FABULOUS FAÇADE** If your venue has a dramatic façade, use that as the backdrop for your entire celebration. Exchange vows on the front steps, then set reception tables in the driveway and add uplighting so all those time-worn details really shine.

TIMELESS AND TRADITIONAL

Timeless, elegant weddings are all about finding the perfect venue, and the classics are recognized as such for a reason! Dramatic and statement-making venues, like stone churches with vaulted ceilings or estates with manicured gardens and sweeping staircases, evoke a feeling of elegance before you've ordered a single centerpiece.

The use of traditional venues also gives your wedding a sense of the history of the place you've chosen, infusing your vows with the love stories of the couples who have said the same words in the same spot before you. By starting with a classic foundation, you can infuse elements of your own aesthetic while still honoring tradition.

CATHEDRAL HALLS If your house of worship is this stunning, keep the details simple with white chairs and flowers to let the architecture really shine.

STATELY EXTERIORS Remember, the outside of your ceremony venue is beautiful, too! In addition to the photographs of your vows, take a few photos by the entrance or on the front steps to capture where all those memories were made. **TAKE THE STAIRS** Never pass up the chance to take portraits on a grand staircase! Whether leading to your ceremony venue or in the lobby of the hotel, it's a photo you'll totally cherish.

"If you go with stylish and classic, you'll never go wrong."

RUSTIC

Natural beauty and simple charm

The beauty of the natural world offers endless
inspiration, whether for the leaf motif on an
engagement band or the theme of a rustic wedding.
A refined rustic style embraces organic elements and
outdoor settings, and may incorporate more DIY flair.
With simple charm, a rustic wedding turns to
salvaged wood, wildflowers, and hand-lettered
signage for a look that is warm and welcoming.

BEAUTIFULLY BOHO

While wedding dresses are often seen as prim and proper, rustic brides will be pleased to see softer skirts, more relaxed silhouettes, and easy layers as they head to the bridal salon. Lace, tulle, and chiffon all come together in gowns that are just as laid-back as they are gorgeous.

Give your accessories just as much attention as your dress to create a look that speaks to who you are. Add a wrap, a cape, or a veil if it suits you, or turn to nontraditional accessories like jackets or hats. Bringing a bit of personality into your wedding day attire will ease that feeling of being a bride atop a wedding cake, making you feel like yourself as you walk down the aisle.

RUSTIC TRAIN Not a "veil" kind of bride? Instead, don a wedding gown with a gorgeous cape and train. You will get all the drama in a modern, bohemian way.

A SOFT DETAILED DRESS Lace is a rustic bride's best friend. Sheer lace sleeves, a scalloped hem, and a soft train are the perfect place for any rustic bride to start her wedding dress search. **NATURAL GLAM** Even sparkling accents are at home at a rustic wedding. Pair subtle embellishments on your wedding gown with soft hair and makeup and simple flowers for a look that's pretty and subdued.

"Style isn't about what you wear, but how: how you wear your dress, how you walk in your shoes, and how you carry yourself. If you do it authentically, you'll always be stylish!"

INCORPORATE NATURE Keep your hairstyle soft and natural by adding a few simple flowers to pulled-back curls. Sprigs of baby's breath—or even a cluster of greenery—is an organic addition to delicate waves. **MAKE IT YOUR OWN** Let your personalities shine through! Put a boho twist on a rustic celebration with a perfectly bridal lace cardigan and a jaunty feather-topped hat.

CROWNING GLORY

There's no accessory better fit for a rustic wedding than a flower crown. These wreaths of blooms nestle delicately above waves and curls, the perfect headpiece for an organic celebration.

If you'd rather wear flowers in your hair than a veil, choose a size and style to fit your particular rustic vision. A crown of full blooms like peonies or garden roses is decidedly bohemian, while a more delicate crown of greenery and small, soft buds like spray roses or lisianthus creates a fairy tale effect.

Play with color and texture to create visual interest, taking cues from the rest of your floral design for a crown that fits seamlessly into the big picture.

SWEET AND SIMPLE Flower crowns don't have to be oversized bohemian affairs. A branch of silver dollar eucalyptus, paired with small textured flowers like sea holly, is a toned-down way for a rustic bride to add an organic touch to her wedding day look. **WREATHED IN GREENS** Treat your flower crown like you would any other floral accessories, tying it back to the details of your bouquet. Use the same greenery that surrounds the flowers you've chosen, and turn to the same blooms for a coordinated style that's absolutely effortless.

"*Let your personal aesthetic shine. Whether it's the color of your dress or your dream flower crown, you should still look—and feel—like you.*"

PRETTY PINS

Rustic boutonnieres are a far cry from prim and manicured classic styles. They incorporate unique and unexpected elements to add color and texture, resulting in a soft and gathered look that fits right in with a rustic aesthetic.

Start by turning to the garden, using fresh herbs or dried grasses to contrast against more traditional flowers. Play with colors that enhance your palette, or keep the arrangement simple and let the wrap do the talking. Jute twine is a go-to at a rustic wedding, but cotton baker's twine (which comes in a variety of colors), ribbons, or hand-dyed silk can also enhance and elevate the handmade look.

LIGHT TEXTURE Strands of dried wheat, pearlescent lunaria leaves, fluffy milkweed, and petite astrantia give this rustic boutonniere tons of organic texture. A white silk ribbon elevates the white-and-green arrangement for an elegant finish.

VIBRANT HUES For a playful pop, swap traditional blooms for vibrant yellow billy balls (also called craspedia). These round flowers are set on sturdy stems without greenery, making them perfect for a boutonniere that's all about color. **GARDEN SPRIGS** Head to the garden for a boutonniere that smells as good as it looks. Pair lavender, rosemary, and thyme for texture and color—the combination of scents will take you back to the moment of your first kiss every time you catch a whiff.

"Dare to be different! A bit of texture from unique and unexpected flowers and greenery can entirely change your look."

PEONY BLOSSOM Soften the rustic look of a tweed vest with a white peony boutonniere. Using the partially closed bud keeps the boutonniere from feeling too large, while the cascading petals create volume and add a bit of romance.

AU NATUREL

The easiest way to instantly give your wedding a rustic feel is to incorporate lots of organic elements and natural texture into your design. These materials, while less polished than their traditional counterparts, help set a tone of relaxation and instantly make your celebration feel homey and lived-in.

Everything from the furniture you choose to how you arrange the flowers can contribute to this final feeling. Look for tables and chairs that are weathered, worn, or unfinished, and consider skipping the tablecloth for a laid-back look. If you are using linens, seek out nubby textures and raw treatments that will feel softer and more relaxed. When it comes to flowers, choose designs that appear just gathered from the garden, using seasonal and flowing elements that are pretty without too much primping. And don't forget the vessels! Vintage or antique vases and bowls help bring the entire look together.

REFINED WOOD Rustic can still feel refined—it's all about the materials you choose. Blonde wood tables and chairs, left uncovered, give this outdoor reception a laid-back garden party vibe, while soft runners and styled centerpieces are subtly sophisticated. **MIXED MATERIALS** Mixed materials instantly loosen up a wedding reception, encouraging guests to settle in and unwind. Galvanized chairs add a metallic pop, while pretty centerpieces get a bit of personality in mismatched vessels ranging from wicker baskets to vintage tins.

LIGHT DÉCOR Soft and loose centerpieces will add a relaxed and rustic ambiance to your reception. Fill a king's table by scattering clustered vases of just-gathered blooms intermittently between printed menus and kraft paper confetti. **SIMPLE ARRANGEMENTS** For a more natural table design, skip the carefully arranged centerpiece in favor of a cluster of bud vases, each holding a single type of bloom. Look for flowers with different textures, like this combination of baby's breath, lavender, and roses. **DRAPED GREENERY** Accent the seats of honor with a garland that's loose and gathered. Pair different types of eucalyptus for a combination of shapes and sizes, all in the plant's iconic muted green tone. **MONOCHROME LINEN** Linens can play a major role in helping set a rustic scene. Woven textures like linen have a natural look that's slightly wrinkled—in a totally chic way. Use cream, ivory, or oatmeal for a soft and organic place setting.

ALTARS & ARCHES

Set your vows against a gorgeous backdrop that will perfectly frame the moment you say "I do." Whether it's a curved arch, an organic wooden frame, or a garden-inspired pergola, the addition of fresh flowers and flowing fabrics will create a can't-miss focal point.

When selecting a ceremony structure, pick a shape and material that fit with both your theme and your venue. A mountain wedding might use birch or aspen branches, while a garden celebration would be the perfect place for a vintage metal arbor. Whatever you select, ensure it's tall enough for the two of you to stand beneath it, and wide enough to fit you both, and your officiant, comfortably.

RUSTIC RUINS When decorating a time-worn space, keep your ceremony set-up equally rustic. Opt for branches instead of a manicured arch, and use cascading flowers in an unfussy shape to bring in a bit of color.

A WOODEN TEPEE For a rustic wedding with a boho vibe, a tepee makes an impressive focal point, especially when coupled with painted stumps for seating.

OUTSIDE AND INTIMATE When celebrating beneath a pergola, add a backdrop of flowing fabric to prevent the ceremony space from feeling too big, keeping you and your partner close to your guests.

OVERHEAD INSTALLATIONS

Dining al fresco beneath a pergola covered in flowers and vines is incredibly romantic, so it's no wonder these rustic installations have made their way into wedding design. Whether you're draping the ceiling of a tent or adding an organic finish to a manicured outdoor space, creating that lived-in feeling can turn a pretty reception into an immersive experience.

To make sure your overhead installation feels rustic, ask your florist to incorporate draped and hanging elements for a more natural and organic finish. Use a variety of textures—such as Italian ruscus, eucalyptus, ferns, and even hop garlands— for a layered look, weaving in fairy lights for a celebration reminiscent of the perfect evening on the patio at dusk.

VINEYARD VINES For a wedding on a vineyard, let your natural surroundings inspire the overhead installation. Here, grape vines are paired with hydrangeas for a display that's perfectly at home.

BULBS AND BLOSSOMS
A room-filling (and ceiling-covering!) installation can be a budget-breaker, but it's a unique accent that's hard to resist. Get a similar look for less by hanging petite bud vases filled with blooms to create an organic statement behind the bar or surrounding the sweetheart table. **FULL AND SUBTLE** When installing flowers and greenery overhead, keep centerpieces low and simple to allow each design to shine without overwhelming. Use pieces from each as an accent in the other, such as the pink roses studded amongst the greenery or the bits of baby's breath tucked into the compotes on the table.

WELCOME SIGNS

A well-informed guest is a happy guest, and all it takes is a little bit of signage to make sure everyone knows what to expect throughout the proceedings.

Wedding signage comes in every style, so choose an option that best fits your theme. For a rustic wedding, turn to engraved wood or chalkboards to continue your relaxed, organic feel. Worried about chalk wiping off? Use vinyl decals that look like handwriting, or opt for white paint with a chalky finish that will stay put, even if someone bumps up against the sign. Top it all off with a garland of greenery and fresh flowers that tie in with your centerpieces.

COCKTAIL POST Whether you've got a mixologist behind the bar or are offering self-serve batch cocktails, a descriptive sign will tempt guests to taste your signature drinks.

"Taking care of your guests is the key to entertaining. Clear signage will let your loved ones know you've taken care of everything."

TIDY CHALK WRITING
Handwritten signage gives a wedding a personal touch. Choose a larger size that guests are sure to spot, and remember to use a ruler to keep lines of text nice and straight.

RUSTIC MEETS MODERN Mix rustic and modern by using clean lines and bold fonts on organic materials, such as this "dessert" sign displayed on a piece of wood. **WITTY PHRASES** What's a wedding without a few clever phrases? Instead of just telling guests where to find their favors, pick a line that speaks to your love and the gift you're handing out. **WHAT'S ON THE MENU?** Displayed dinner menus are perfect for family-style or buffet meals. A sign also means you will save on the cost of printing out individual menus for everyone in attendance.

NAKED CAKES

Rustic weddings are worn around the edges in the most enchanting way, making naked cakes the perfect dessert to end a warm, relaxed, and inviting evening. These cakes peel away the fuss of fondant, letting the best bites do all the talking.

Naked cakes are still full of finesse, as the cake and frosting are on full display for all to see. If you're considering going bare with your cake, talk to your baker about any steps he or she might take to keep the cake extra moist, and make sure you love the look of each flavor as much as you love the taste. Then add in a few fresh flowers, and you're ready for that first sweet bite as newlyweds!

SEMI-NAKED For a frosting-lover who wants the rustic look of a naked cake, opt for a semi-naked design. Buttercream, smoothed around the outside of each tier, is gently removed to let the layers shine through while still giving a sweet finish to every bite.

SINGLE SERVINGS
Individual ombré naked cakes? This dessert display is three trends in one, and the addition of fresh flowers and greenery ties it together perfectly. Matching the colors of the cake with the colors of the flowers is eye-catching attention to detail.

DRESS IT UP Every cake needs a little dressing up, and the garlands of greenery and spray roses around each tier of this naked cake give it a relaxed, just-picked finish and add a bit of polish to a rustic design.

SOMETHING SWEET

Why serve just cake when you can treat your guests to an indulgent spread of after-dinner sweets? Laden down a table with a selection of your favorite desserts, from cupcakes and tartlets to brownies and trifles.

Give the design of your dessert table a little extra thought—after all, it will absolutely be a focal point of your reception. Whether you choose pretty trays, mix in petite floral arrangements, or design a grand display using flowers and décor items to transform that corner of your space, those little details will catch guests' attention and make sure every last sweet is eaten. Just remember to set a few aside in a box for you and your new spouse to enjoy once the festivities are over.

BITE-SIZED To keep a dessert table feeling rustic and refined—not messy—opt for individual desserts with a neat presentation. Miniature trifles, bite-sized tarts, and other polished treats will feel relaxed but look enticing.

DECORATIVE STANDS Incorporate different levels to lure guests in to an indulgent dessert display. Boxes, stands, and cake plates will elevate the sweets you've chosen, giving each a moment to shine.

EASY AS PIE As with appetizers, the most successful dessert tables are laden with one- or two-bite treats that are easy to eat. These pie pops pack all the flavor of a slice, no plate or fork required.
SWEET SURROUNDINGS Create an environment around your dessert display to catch guests' eyes. Flowers or plants create an organic feel, while a neon sign against warn barn wood is a fresh modern-meets-rustic contrast.
GALVANIZED DISPLAY Pick materials that speak to your theme, from galvanized metal to slices of logs, and use those same materials throughout your wedding design.

"Taking the time to carefully arrange a table is an expression of care toward the people you have invited to celebrate with you."

VINTAGE

The best of the past today

The styles of yesteryear are full of inspiration for
a contemporary wedding. Whether it's a gorgeously
beaded bridal gown in the Art Nouveau style or a
classic 1950s roadster, past eras offer visions of beauty
that can make a wedding unique and sensational.
Like an Art Deco inspired ring, a vintage wedding
is distinctive and refined.

LOVELY LACE

Vintage and lace go hand-in-hand, and most brides looking to the past for inspiration will find themselves drawn to lace elements when shopping for their wedding gowns. But there's more to lace than meets the eye! This intricate fabric comes in endless patterns, so you can choose a lace that best fits your style. From floral to modern, simple to embellished, there is a lace for every aesthetic.

Think about where and how the lace is used, too. Head-to-toe lace gowns are feminine and sweet, while overlays on sleeves or necklines can add an alluring sheer accent to a more traditional silhouette. Beading and crystals add sparkle and shine—though lace looks equally lovely with or without the sparkle. Some dresses also combine multiple styles of lace, using larger patterns alongside more delicate trim designs for a geometric look or a figure-flattering cut.

The best way to find the right lace for you? Try on a variety of styles until one jumps out as "The One"— just like your soon-to-be spouse.

SCALLOPED PATTERNS
Because guests will spend most of the ceremony looking at your back, pick a dress that has a little something for them to look at until it's time for your first kiss. This scalloped lace pattern goes from head to toe, but the sheer back panel shows a little something without being too revealing. **UPDATED LACE NECKLINE** A beautiful lace sleeve is a vintage bride's dream. To bring this more conservative style into the modern era, look for a v-neck back (instead of the high necks of yore) and a more modern floral pattern. **WEAVE IN PEARLS** Nothing goes together quite like lace and pearls. To give your dress a bit of vintage oomph, look for delicate pearl beading along the edges of the lace pattern to set the style apart. **LIGHTENED-UP LACE** High-neck gowns don't need to be stuffy. Lighten up the covered-up look with a few sheer panels, either sitting directly on your skin or over a nude underlay. These graphic elements make a traditional lace bodice feel unique. **SHORT AND SWEET** Who says wedding dresses have to be long? Whether you are heading to City Hall or having a large reception with loved ones, a knee-length skirt covered in lace has a sweet and retro disposition.

"Style used to define us, but today we can choose our own style—so select one that makes you feel your very best."

COUPLE'S STYLE

When selecting attire for a vintage wedding, make sure both of your outfits are drawing inspiration from the same era. Nothing throws off a theme like fashion from decades apart!

For men, a tuxedo will always be a classic, with a vest or tails transforming it for an earlier time period and a more traditional style making the look more contemporary. If you're donning a suit, pick a color that was popular during the time—brown and tan suits are inherently vintage. Add accessories like suspenders or a bow tie to complete the look.

Women's fashion is easier to give a vintage flare. Don't be afraid of unique fabrics or a little color—remember that white wedding dresses weren't always de rigueur!

DECIDEDLY VINTAGE
Post-War style is all about finding the very best items from your grandmother's closet. A faux-fur stole, birdcage veil, and suit with elbow patches would be right at home in that family album.

PLAY WITH HUES Turn-of-the-century fashion is defined by nipped waists and column skirts. A high-neck blouse, full sleeve, barely blue hue, and lots of lace are decidedly feminine.

BEST TRESSED

Your dress may be the biggest decision you make regarding your wedding day look, but your hairstyle is just as important. Choosing the right 'do can go a long way in enhancing your wedding style, especially if you're having a vintage-inspired celebration.

Turn to fashion photography and magazines from the past to figure out how you'd like to style your locks, as well as find ideas for hair accessories and headpieces that will bring it all together. Brides turning to turn-of-the-century weddings for inspiration will love a full chignon of soft curls, while those inspired by the Art Deco era will be drawn to finger waves. Be sure to schedule a trial with your hair stylist so you can make sure you love the results, and tweak the style if needed.

LACY HEIRLOOM Heirlooms are a meaningful way to incorporate those closest to you into your wedding day, and vintage celebrations make it even easier. Ask your mother or grandmother to lend you a wedding-day accessory, such as a headpiece or hair comb, to bring a bit of the past down the aisle with you.

STATEMENT HEADPIECE
No veil? No problem. Accent a soft updo with a swirling lace headpiece that perfectly matches your gown for a sweet and simple statement.

REPURPOSED BROOCH
Vintage jewelry is incredibly versatile, and all it takes is a few carefully placed bobby pins to turn a beautiful brooch into the perfect accent for a pile of curls. Look for a piece with an ornate and elongated shape that can rest just above your hairstyle.

"Whether you call it retro, vintage, or antique, turn to styles and accessories of the past to bring your vintage wedding day ensemble together."

FLAPPER MAIDS Give your bridesmaids' hairstyles a vintage flare, too. For an Art Deco evening, turn to flapper style and add beaded headpieces and soft feathers to finger waves. Finish it all off with bold red lipstick.

ENDURING ACCESSORIES

What's old is new again, as vintage style has made its way back into contemporary fashion. These classic and beloved details, from a string of pearls to the perfect satin shoe, are getting a modern interpretation.

The beauty of donning a vintage accessory is the instant connection to brides of the past—mothers, grandmothers, and great-grandmothers who also wore pearls or chose lace dresses, and who may have passed those very pieces down to you. If there was ever a wedding designed for "something borrowed," it's one with a vintage theme. Let heirloom wedding photos be your guide as you define your style to give your vintage attire a sense of history and authenticity.

BRIDAL BUTTONS Is there anything more striking than a row of satin-covered buttons down the back of a wedding gown? This simple detail instantly gives a dress a vintage aesthetic, and those moments as your loved ones fasten the buttons are ones you'll never forget.

"Vintage style has a feeling of nostalgia and romance, a sense of the past given new meaning in our modern lexicon."

HEIRLOOM JEWELS Whether you've borrowed earrings from your grandmother's jewelry box or purchased a pair with the past in mind, combining the tones of yellow gold and warm champagne give a classic accessory a vintage feeling. **HAND-BEADED DETAILS** If you don't love wearing jewelry but still want to sparkle on your wedding day, look for a wedding dress with crystals or beading around the neckline. It will add delicate and feminine shine, and when placed on an illusion neckline, can look just like jewelry—but it won't budge all night! **SATIN AND PEARLS** Brides have been wearing white satin shoes and a strand of pearls down the aisle for decades, so don't mess with a good thing. If you don't have access to real pearls, seek out a faux variety with a polished and authentic look—no one will know the difference.

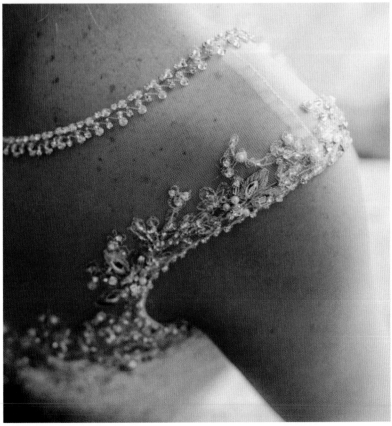

SUIT UP

Transform a group of groomsmen into dashing gentlemen with the perfect vintage attire and accessories. When carefully selected and properly tailored, these outfits will feel comfortable and easy—a far cry from the costumes you might have been picturing.

Pair modern silhouettes, such as slim pants and expertly tapered waists, with a vintage palette, fabric, or accessories to keep your suit feeling fresh. Not ready to invest in a new suit? Many rental companies offer vintage-inspired options (such as seersucker, tan suits, and three-piece options) so you can build a look that fits your wedding inspiration. Then turn to accessories to personalize every detail: bowties, vests, pocket squares, and suspenders were all staples in a bygone era, and your wedding day is the perfect opportunity to bring them back.

RETRO PATTERNS There's something about seersucker that harkens back to the '20s and '30s, with men in light suits and women in white dresses playing croquet on the lawn. Bring that breezy summer vibe and retro twist to your wedding with a striped and textured suit of your own.

A PERFECT FIT When well-tailored, a suit with a unique texture and subtle pattern can seamlessly walk the line between vintage and modern. Contrasting wooden buttons and a white bowtie—plus a patterned pocket square—are decidedly dapper.

VINTAGE COLORS A three-piece suit in warm brown will look straight from your grandfather's closet, in a good way. This chocolate-hued ensemble could have walked straight off the set of a period drama, giving your vintage wedding a true sense of time. **ADD SUSPENDERS** Three accessories come together to make a suit immediately feel vintage: a vest, a bowtie, and suspenders. These pieces are a great way to add personality (and maybe a pop of color!) to a groom's wedding day look. **ACCESSORIZE** Pocket watches are as vintage as they come. Carry a family heirloom down the aisle, or purchase vintage-inspired and engraved versions as gifts for the most important men in your life.

ART DECO FLAIR

The Art Deco period of the 1920s and 1930s is full of design inspiration to give your wedding a modern-meets-vintage vibe. From sharp lines and geometric shapes to cascading pearls and lots of sparkle, there's a creative detail or playful accent everywhere you look.

As you're bringing Art Deco to the modern era, choose a few vintage-inspired details and make them your focus. By subtly weaving Deco sensibility into a more contemporary setting, you can create an elegant evening inspired by a bygone era—but avoid the feeling of a costume party. Stay consistent, using those same design elements throughout your décor, to transport guests to another time in high style.

A MODERN FLAPPER Outfit a flower girl in a playful frock with a fun and vintage vibe. Sequins give this dress girlish sparkle, while the scalloped shape finishes off the Art Deco feel.

GRAPHIC ELEMENTS OF OLD
Paper goods are the perfect place to incorporate Art Deco design. Let posters, artwork, and even architecture inspire your invitation design, using those same shapes on cocktail napkins, signage, and even your cake!

LAYERED JEWELS Art Deco fashion is synonymous with layers of cascading pearls, but make it modern by draping jewels down your back, instead. It's still perfectly on-theme, while creating a show-stopping look that's right at home in the modern era. **SOFT FEATHERY FINISHES** A round bouquet of roses is a total classic, but the addition of white peacock feathers and a few scabiosa pods gives this floral arrangement a graphic Art Deco finish.

CHARMING GARDEN PARTY

Embrace the magic and nostalgia of a bygone era at a vintage garden party. Pair lush blooms, cozy vignettes, and lots of bubbly for a wedding in the garden that's a real celebration.

To keep the vintage vibe alive, select statement pieces of antique furniture and décor and treat them as a focal point, whether at the altar, behind the bar, or scattered throughout cocktail hour. Offer classic cocktails as a jazz trio plays in the shade, and set out a game of croquet for some post-ceremony fun. Take a cue from the best Jazz Age hosts and hostesses, making sure your guests are smiling, drinks are full, and everyone is ready for the party ahead.

VICTORIAN VIGNETTE Lounge vignettes create welcoming places for guests to gather—and the perfect spot for a few photos. Carefully placed umbrellas, garlands of balloons and palm fronds, and woven peacock chairs put a tropical spin on a vintage celebration. **GARDEN PERGOLA** An intricate metal pergola is charmingly old-school, a lovely space to prop table assignments and frame your wedding cake. Guests will love using the twinkling frame as a background for photographs.

VINTAGE BAR CART Raise a glass! Pour some bubbly (or a sugar-rimmed champagne cocktail) and set out bar carts to encourage guests to help themselves as they wander through the garden. **BYGONE BAR** Bring the indoors out with residential inspired furnishings. A stately bar will remind guests of the way people entertained in days gone by, as well as create a can't-miss focal point for cocktail hour.

RETRO ROMANCE

Vintage doesn't always mean Victorian. The '40s and '50s are full of colorful and creative inspiration that can give your wedding celebration a retro-chic feel.

Design from this era spans mid-century modern, organic, and even early hints of pop, so you can really narrow down the style that speaks to you. Get creative with color, go wild with unique furniture rentals, and take your time choosing the perfect accessories so even your attire is on-theme. Whether you're drawn to soft curves, sharp angles, or the most vibrant of hues, designing a retro wedding is all about finding an aesthetic that feels perfectly you.

"From the fashion to the flatware, let your chosen era inspire every detail of your wedding for a beautiful big picture."

OPEN-TOE PUMPS Accessories are the icing on the cake. For a retro finish, don peep toe pumps with a sweet bow peeking out from beneath your gown. Bonus points for a touch of sparkle! **VINTAGE BAR CART** Nothing says Mad Men quite like a mobile bar. Add in a custom neon sign to personalize cocktail hour even more. **RETRO GLASSWARE** Don't forget what's behind the bar. Unique glassware with a vintage vibe, whether it's colored crystal goblets or mod and angular lowballs, will help tell your story.

EMBRACE MIS-MATCHED
Make mismatched work for you. A curated collection of vintage-style chairs makes kitschy design oh-so-cool.
TEXTURED TABLE-SCAPES
Keep that texture going on your tabletop. Pair patterned linens with vases, vessels, and glassware in a variety of shapes and colors for a layered look—just keep the flowers consistent so it still feels polished. **PASTELS OF PAST** Ruffled peach roses and white hydrangeas give this bouquet a sweet, vintage feel. Seeded eucalyptus and green poppy pods add a modern flare. **ECLECTIC BOUQUET** Use your bouquet as your "something blue" by adding hydrangeas and sea holly to a cluster of roses and cotton buds.

THE GOLDEN AGE OF INVITATIONS

A vintage wedding can draw inspiration from any number of eras, so use the design elements in your invitation suite to let guests know which time period you'll be turning to for your wedding day.

Three eras are the most-turned-to when it comes to wedding design. Art Nouveau, from the late 19th and early 20th centuries, uses elongated lines and curves inspired by botany—look for a suite with subtle floral details and swirling lines. Art Deco, from the 1920s to the 1940s, emphasizes geometric forms and straight lines, paired with metallics and bold colors—easily translated into an invitation suite. Mid-Century Modern, popular from the 1930s to the 1960s, turns to simple and structural shapes, sleek angles, and natural materials paired with futuristic designs—a fitting suite would have geometric shapes and a retro palette.

Whichever era inspires you, use these elements to transport your guests to another time.

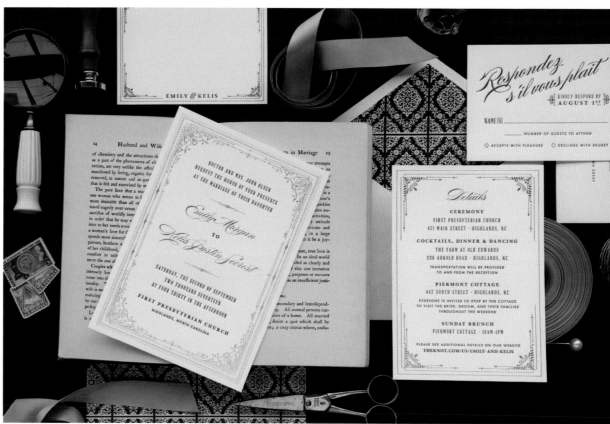

BOLD SHAPES AND STRONG COLORS Warm gold and graphic accents give this invitation suite an Art Deco feel. The clean lines and sharp shapes are reminiscent of 1920s architecture, while a variety of typefaces add visual drama to an otherwise simple design. **INTRICATE DESIGN** For an invitation that's more Art Nouveau, turn to intricate and undulating borders with subtly organic elements. Give the pattern punch by having it embossed into your suite, and select an ornamental envelope liner to tie this detailed style together.

together with their families

Alexandria Maninos
and
Malcom Davidson III

request the pleasure of your company
on the occasion of their wedding

Saturday, the eleventh of June
two thousand and sixteen
at half past five o'clock in the evening

Dover Hall Estate
Manakin-Sabot, Virginia

cocktails, dinner and dancing to follow

Responde Sil
Vous Plait

M_____

graciously accepts   respectfully declines

Mr. Mrs.
Malcom Davidson
402 Larchmont Cres.
Norfolk, Virginia

Merci
Beaucoup

A DOILY SLEEVE Delicate line
drawings and an unexpected
envelope make this invitation
feel right out of the past.
Wrap each suite in a vintage
handkerchief, then tuck the
whole thing into a larger
envelope for a presentation
that will truly wow your guests.

Index

Photo Credits

The publisher would like to thank the following for their kind permission to reproduce their photographs:
(Key: a-above; b-below/bottom; c-center; f-far; l-left; r-right; t-top)

Front cover ©NEIL LANE COUTURE™. **9** Dorling Kindersley: Carolyn Barber. **10–11** Shutterstock: Jonathan Ball. **13** ©Christopher Malcom.
16 Stocksy: Seth Mourra (l). ©Andrew Bayda (r). **17** ©Sean Cook Weddings (l)(r). **19** ©Sean Cook Weddings (t). Shutterstock: Pavlo Melnyk (b).
20 Stocksy: Leah Flores (l). Stocksy: Seth Mourra (r). **23** ©Shannon Moffit Photography. **24** Stocksy: Seth Mourra. **25** Shutterstock: Andrey
Nastasenko (t). ©Anna Delores Photography (b). **26–27** Stocksy: Anwyn Howarth. **28** ©Shannon Moffit Photography (r)(l). **29** ©Shannon Moffit
Photography (t)(cl)(cr)(b). **30** ©Shannon Moffit Photography (tl)(tr)(cla)(cra)(clb)(crb)(br). Shutterstock: Siarhei Arynokhin (bl). **31** Stocksy:
Dreamwood – Michael & Lucy (t). Stocksy: Seth Mourra (b). **32** Shutterstock: aprilante (t). ©Peyton Rainey Photography (c). Stocksy: Adrian
Cotiga (b). **34** ©Anna Delores Photography. **35** ©Anna Delores Photography (t). Stocksy: Seth Mourra (bl). ©Kristen Booth (br). **40** ©Shannon
Moffit Photography. **41** ©Anna Delores Photography. **42** ©Anna Delores Photography. **44** ©Shannon Moffit Photography (l). ©Andrew Bayda (r)
45 ©Andrew Bayda. **48** ©Lauren Kearns. **49** ©Lauren Kearns. **50** Stocksy: Liliya Rodnikova. **51** Lauren Kearns. **52** Stocksy: Leah Flores (l).
©Shannon Moffit Photography (r). **53** Stocksy: Dreamwood – Michael & Lucy (l). Anna Delores Photography (r). **55** ©Sean Cook Weddings (t)(br)
(bl). **56** ©Shannon Moffit Photography (t)(b). **57** Stocksy: Marta Locklear. **58** Stocksy: Cameron Whitman (l). ©Sean Cook Weddings (r).
59 Stocksy: Seth Mourra. **61** Stocksy: Seth Mourra. **62** ©Anna Delores Photography. **63** Dorling Kindersley: John Davis (tl). Dorling Kindersley:
Dave King (tc). Dorling Kindersley: Brian North/RHS Chelsea Flower Show 2012 (tr). Dorling Kindersley: Carolyn Barber (bl). Dorling Kindersley:
Mark Winwood (bc). Dorling Kindersley: Clive Streeter (br). **65** Stocksy: Susan Findlay (tl). Dorling Kindersley: Clare West (tr). ©Gabrielle Cheikh
(bl). Shutterstock: Valery Petrushkov (br). **66** Stocksy: Andrew Cebulka (t). Stocksy: Seth Mourra (cl)(b). Stocksy: Marta Locklear (cr). **67** Dorling
Kindersley: Gary Ombler (tl). Shutterstock: haru (tc). Stocksy: Sonya Khegay (tr). Dorling Kindersley: Steve Gorton (bl). Dorling Kindersley: Gary
Ombler (bc). Dorling Kindersley: Sian Irvine (br). **69** ©Gabrielle Cheikh. **70** Stocksy: Duet Postscriptum. **71** Shutterstock: Sergey Melnikov (tl).
Stocksy: Kirill Bordon Photography (tr). ©Gabrielle Cheikh (b). **73** Stocksy: Seth Mourra. **74** Dorling Kindersley: Tony Souter. **75** ©Sean Cook
Weddings. **76** Stocksy: Seth Mourra. **77** ©Anna Delores Photography. **78** Stocksy: Christian Gideon (t). Stocksy: Vicki Grafton Photography (b).
79 Stocksy: Seth Mourra. **80** Shutterstock: onejulyphotography. **81** ©Anna Delores Photography (t). ©Anna Delores Photography (b). **82** Stocksy:
Duet Postscriptum. **83** Stocksy: Wendy Laurel. **84** Shutterstock: Alexander Baitelman. **85** ©Shannon Moffit Photography. **86** Stocksy: Ani Dimi.
86–87 Unsplash: Sweet Ice Cream Photography. **91** ©KAY® Jewelers. **92** Stocksy: Seth Mourra. **93** Stocksy: Ania Boniecka (l). ©Kristen Booth (tr).
Stocksy: Seth Mourra (br). **94** Stocksy: Milles Studio. **95** Stocksy: Seth Mourra (tl). Stocksy: Lyuba Burakova (tr)(b). **96** Stocksy: Seth Mourra (r).
©Shannon Moffit Photography (l). **97** Stocksy: Julia K (l). ©Lauren Kearns (r). **98** ©Anna Delores Photography. **99** Stocksy: Kirill Bordon
Photography (l). ©Kelsea Holder (r). **100** Stocksy: Seth Mourra (t). ©Sean Cook Weddings (b). **101** Shutterstock: Andrey Nastasenko (t). Stocksy:
Julia K (bl). Stocksy: Seth Mourra (br). **102** ©Shannon Moffit Photography. **103** ©Anna Delores Photography. **104** ©Sean Cook Weddings (t).
©Kristen Booth (b). **105** Stocksy: Seth Mourra (l). ©Sean Cook Weddings (r). **106** Stocksy: Evgeniya Savina (t). Stocksy: Seth Mourra (b).
107 Stocksy: Seth Mourra (l). Dorling Kindersley: Charlotte Tolhurst (r). **108** Stocksy: Thais Ramos Varela. **109** ©Ella K Photography (tl). Stocksy:
Alicia Magnuson Photography (tr). Shutterstock: ludovicabastianini (b). **111** ©KAY® Jewelers. **112–113** StockSnap: Chirobocea Nicu. **114** ©Genevieve
Nisly Photography (t). iStock: freemixer (b). **115** ©Lauren Kearns (l). Stocksy: Kristen Curette Hines (r). **116–117** ©Kristen Booth. **118** ©Andrew
Bayda. **119** Stocksy: Dreamwood – Michael & Lucy (t). ©Andrew Bayda (b). **120** Genevieve Nisly Photography (l). Stacy Marks (r). **121** ©Andrew
Bayda (l). Genevieve Nisly Photography (r). **122** ©All Bliss Photography. **123** ©All Bliss Photography. **124** ©Andrew Bayda. **125** ©Perez
Photography (t). ©Shea Christine (b). **126** Adobe Stock: Maria Sbytova. **127** ©Kristen Booth (tl)(tr). Stocksy: Seth Mourra (bl). ©Dahlia Press (br).
128 Stocksy: Evgeniya Savina (c)(r). **129** Stocksy: Evgeniya Savina (t)(br). Stocksy: Thais Ramos Varela (bl). **131** ©KAY® Jewelers. **132** Stocksy:
Studio Firma (l). ©Ivy Road Photography (r). **133** ©Sean Cook Weddings (l). ©Andrew Bayda (r). **134** ©Sean Cook Weddings (t). Shutterstock:
Alexander Voight (b). **135** ©Anna Delores Photography (l)(r). **136** Shutterstock: Andrey Nastasenko. **137** Shutterstock: Kate Kultsevych (t). Adobe
Stock: photographmd (b). **138** Stocksy: Leah Flores (l). Stocksy: Seth Mourra (r). **139** ©Highlight Studios (l). Stocksy: Andrew Cebulka (r).
140 ©Anna Delores Photography. **141** ©Anna Delores Photography (tl) ©Ella K Photography (tr). Stocksy: Dreamwood – Michael & Lucy (b).
142 ©Anna Delores Photography. **143** ©Benjamin David Photography (l). Stocksy: Seth Mourra (r). **144** Unsplash: Kelly Neil. **145** Stocksy: Seth
Mourra (tl). Shutterstock: Sasha Lee Photography (tr). Stocksy: Seth Mourra (bl). ©Anna Delores Photography (br). **146** Stocksy: Seth Mourra (l).
©Anna Delores Photography (r). **147** Stocksy: Seth Mourra (l)(r). **148** Stocksy: Seth Mourra. **149** ©Kelsea Holder (t). ©Lauren Fair Photography
(b). **150** Stocksy: Seth Mourra. **151** Stocksy: Jess Craven. **153** ©KAY® Jewelers. **154–155** Highlight Studios. **156** Stocksy: Dreamwood – Michael &
Lucy. **157** ©Lauren Kearns (l). ©Shannon Moffit Photography (r). **158** ©Lauren Kearns (t). ©Anna Delores Photography (b). **159** ©Lauren Kearns
(l). Stocksy: Seth Mourra (r). **160** ©Lauren Kearns. **161** ©Sean Cook Weddings (l)(r). **162** Stocksy: Seth Mourra. **163** ©Lauren Kearns. **164** Stocksy:
Seth Mourra. **165** ©Anna Delores Photography (tl). Dorling Kindersley: Carolyn Barber (bl). Unsplash: Shelbey Miller (r). **166** Stocksy: Seth

219

Mourra (l). Stocksy: Sidney Morgan (r). **167** ©Lauren Kearns (tl)(tr)(b). **168** Stocksy: Seth Mourra. **169** Stocksy: Seth Mourra (tl)(tr)(bl)(br). **170** Stocksy: Julia K. **171** ©Sean Cook Weddings (tl)(b). Stocksy: Vicki Grafton Photography (tr). **172–173** iStock: Digital Storm. **174** ©Ella K Photography (l). Stocksy: Andreas Gradin (r). **175** ©KAY® Jewelers. **176** ©Shannon Moffit Photography. **177** Stocksy: Jess Craven (tl). Stocksy: Leah Flores (tr). Stocksy: Ania Boniecka (bl). Anna Delores Photography (br). **178** Stocksy: Seth Mourra. **179** ©Alice + Chris. **180** Stocksy: Seth Mourra. **181** Stocksy: Leah Flores (tl). Stocksy: Anjali Pinto (tr). Shutterstock: Alex Gukalov (b). **182** Stocksy: Seth Mourra (t). Stocksy: Lexia Frank (b). **183** Stocksy: Seth Mourra (tl). Unsplash: Photos by Lanty (tr). ©Sean Cook Weddings (bl). Stocksy: Svanberggrath (br). **184** Stocksy: Jess Craven. **185** ©Ivy Road Photography (l). Stocksy: Brat Co. (r). **186** ©Shannon Moffit Photography. **187** Stocksy: Seth Mourra (l). Shutterstock: IVASHstudio (r). **188** Stocksy: Leah Flores (t)(b). **189** Stocksy: Jess Craven (t)(br). ©Gabrielle Cheikh (bl). **190** ©Anna Delores Photography. **191** Unsplash: Thomas AE (l). Shutterstock: Melnikov Sergey (r). **192** Stocksy: Seth Mourra (l). Stocksy: Milles Studio (r). **193** Stocksy: Marta Locklear (t). ©Anna Delores Photography (bl). ©Gabrielle Cheikh (br). **195** ©KAY® Jewelers. **196** Shutterstock: gkondratenko (l). Stocksy: Seth Mourra (r). **197** ©Gabrielle Cheikh (tl). Stocksy: Jess Woodhouse (tr). ©Andrew Bayda (b). **198** Stocksy: Milles Studio. **199** Stocksy: Milles Studio. **200** ©Gabrielle Cheikh. **201** ©Ivy Road Photography (tl)(b). ©Katherine Fawssett (tr). **202** ©Gabrielle Cheikh. **203** ©Gabrielle Cheikh (t). Stocksy: Studio Firma (bl). ©Alice + Chris (br). **204** ©Sean Cook Weddings (t). Stocksy: Chelsea Victoria (b). **205** Unsplash: Alvin Mahmudov (t). ©Anna Delores Photography (bl). ©Gabrielle Cheikh (br). **206** Stocksy: Laura Stolfi (t). ©Lauren Kearns (b). **207** ©Ivy Road Photography (l). ©Lauren Kearns (r). **208** Stocksy: Seth Mourra (l)(r). **209** Stocksy: Seth Mourra (l)(r). **210** Stocksy: Seth Mourra (t). ©Anna Delores Photography (bl)(br). **211** ©Anna Delores Photography (tr)(tl). Stocksy: Ania Boniecka (bl). Shutterstock: Alex Gukalov (br). **212** ©Dahlia Press (t)(b). **213** ©Shannon Moffit Photography. **219** Stocksy: Seth Mourra (l). Stocksy: Dreamwood – Michael & Lucy (c). ©Anna Delores Photography (r). **217** Unsplash: Nyana Stocia. **221** Unsplash: Shelbey Miller. **Back cover** ©Christopher Malcom.

The publisher would like to thank the following for their contributions:

23 Planner: Amore Events by Cody; Venue: Pippin Hill; Florist: Blue Ridge Floral Design. **28** Planner: Pam Olson; Venue: Avalon Palm Springs; Florist: The Bloomin Gypsy; Rentals: Pow Wow Design Studio (l)(r). **29** Planner: Ciera Pope; Venue: Market at Grelen; Florist: Nature Composed (t)(cl)(cr)(b). **30** Stylist: Luxe and Luna (tl)(tr)(crb)(clb). **37** Paper goods curtesy of Paper Source. **38** Copperplate calligraphy: Calligraphy Quill. Modern calligraphy: Tied and Two. Monoline lettering: Adriane Sam Lettering. **39** Pen lettering: Tied and Two. Brush lettering: Tied and Two. **40** Planner: Pam Olson; Venue: Avalon Palm Springs; Florist: The Bloomin Gypsy; Rentals: Pow Wow Design Studio. **44** Planner: Amorology; Venue: Darlington House; Florist: Plenty of Petals (l). **56** Planner: Amore Events by Cody; Venue: Pippin Hill; Florist: Photosynthesis (t). **85** Planner: Amorology; Venue: Darlington House; Florist: Plenty of Petals. **102** Stylist: Luxe and Luna. **157** Planner: Candy Borales; Florist: Suha Kaidbey (r). **176** Stylist: Luxe and Luna. **186** Planner: Amore Events by Cody; Venue: Pippin Hill; Florist: Blue Ridge Floral Design. **203** Hair comb: Agnes Hart.

About the Author

Neil Lane is a celebrated designer, collector, curator, and bridal authority woven into Hollywood's DNA. With an eye for style and elegance, Lane is a jewelry expert and an avid collector of rare jewels, sculptures, and fine art. He shares his unique aesthetic with his fans and customers around the world with his Neil Lane Bridal® collection at Kay® Jewelers. From the moment a couple makes their commitment official, Lane is part of their love story. He makes his mark beginning at the engagement, throughout the planning phases, on the wedding day, and beyond.

Acknowledgments

Much like a wedding, this book would not have been possible without the hard work of so many to whom I'd be remiss not to give thanks. To my partners at Authentic Brands Group—your tenacity to drive a concept from ideation to fruition and your tireless pursuit of perfection have truly helped this project come to life. To my agent, Rick Richter, and publisher, DK Publishing—the words "thank you" don't seem like enough. Your unwavering support and encouragement during the writing process has meant the world to me.

Visuals convey feelings where words fall short—Girl Friday Productions, thank you for the integral role you have played to do just that. To my writing partner, Jaimie Mackey—our conversations that went well beyond the scope of this project have been some of my most cherished times in this process. Thank you for your wisdom, insight, and way with words.

To my family and friends—those who kept me grounded throughout the process—this book simply would not have been possible without you. Most importantly, I would like to thank all of you—my readers. You are about to embark on an extraordinary chapter in your life, and I am thrilled to be a page in your journey.